Options Installment Strategies

Michael C. Thomsett

Options Installment Strategies

Long-Term Spreads for Profiting from Time Decay

palgrave
macmillan

Michael C. Thomsett
Spring Hill, TN, USA

ISBN 978-3-319-99863-3   ISBN 978-3-319-99864-0 (eBook)
https://doi.org/10.1007/978-3-319-99864-0

Library of Congress Control Number: 2018962267

© The Editor(s) (if applicable) and The Author(s), under exclusive licence to Springer Nature Switzerland AG 2018
This work is subject to copyright. All rights are solely and exclusively licensed by the Publisher, whether the whole or part of the material is concerned, specifically the rights of translation, reprinting, reuse of illustrations, recitation, broadcasting, reproduction on microfilms or in any other physical way, and transmission or information storage and retrieval, electronic adaptation, computer software, or by similar or dissimilar methodology now known or hereafter developed.
The use of general descriptive names, registered names, trademarks, service marks, etc. in this publication does not imply, even in the absence of a specific statement, that such names are exempt from the relevant protective laws and regulations and therefore free for general use.
The publisher, the authors and the editors are safe to assume that the advice and information in this book are believed to be true and accurate at the date of publication. Neither the publisher nor the authors or the editors give a warranty, express or implied, with respect to the material contained herein or for any errors or omissions that may have been made. The publisher remains neutral with regard to jurisdictional claims in published maps and institutional affiliations.

Cover image © Scar1984 / iStock / Getty Images Plus
Cover design by Oscar Spigolon

This Palgrave Macmillan imprint is published by the registered company Springer Nature Switzerland AG
The registered company address is: Gewerbestrasse 11, 6330 Cham, Switzerland

Preface: Why a *Contingent* Method?

Options are flexible and can be matched to any risk profile.

The potential for options trading covers the entire risk spectrum. You can trade as a speculator, taking great risks and hoping to reap great rewards. Or you can proceed as a conservative investor interested in preserving the value of an equity portfolio and eliminating market risk.

For example, whereas a speculator is attracted to uncovered calls in highly volatile markets, a buy-and-hold investor must be concerned with volatility in price, and with the basic requirement of meeting or exceeding a breakeven level. Considering the combination of inflation and taxes, achieving breakeven is difficult and may require taking higher risks than you prefer. This problem is unavoidable. Doing nothing means your spending power is eroded. Taking higher risks means you increase exposure and risk losses you cannot afford.

Options are the solution. However, it is not enough to trade options on an underlying stock without some form of qualification. An investing philosophy applied in this approach is that qualifying a company as a first step is an absolute requirement. A fundamentally strong company sees its strength translated to the stock price, and in turn this makes options stronger and less risky. In first selecting stocks of high quality, you begin the journey of options trading with confidence that the options strategies you employ are more likely to yield profits, and less likely to experience losses resulting from volatility.

A *contingent* method of trading is one way to use options for risk reduction, while enabling a long-term "layaway" for stock purchase at a fixed price, or a long-term risk hedge that eliminates market risk.

An installment call involves fixing today's price per share for as long as two and a half years. If you want to buy stock in the future but you are not sure the price will rise, the installment call is the solution, fixing the price today for a small portion of the cost of buying stock. An installment put protects you if you already own shares. The long-term put freezes market risk at the put's strike, so that any price movement below that level is offset by value in the put. This use of options is among the most effective methods of portfolio management.

These hedging mechanisms are designed for any investor who recognizes the need to protect the portfolio for many years into the future. Whether investing as an individual or an institutional manager, the contingent method of options trading is low risk and designed to either fix the price of a future purchase or eliminate risk of shares already owned. Many options publications have discussed the use of long-term options, or LEAPS (long-term equity anticipation securities), as an alternative to options expiring within a few weeks or months. However, what has lacked in previous discussion of LEAPS trading is the methodology for using these options to eliminate risk or to fix prices for future trading. Also missing has been any discussion of how to buy a LEAPS call or put and pay for it, so the net basis in the long position is reduced to zero.

This book addresses these questions and demonstrates that a plan of action to do both—using LEAPS as a risk hedge and reducing the basis to zero—with a set of strategies designed to keep risks to a minimum ensure long-term success in hedging and devise a recovery plan in those instances when the plan does not work perfectly.

Why is a recovery plan needed? The answer is based in reality: no trading strategy will work 100 percent of the time. The contingent plan for LEAPS calls or puts has a specific goal and if all goes according to that plan, it succeeds. However, as a trader you also need to prepare for the worst-case outcome. There will be times when the plan has a setback. This is true for all investing. If you buy high-quality stocks paying exceptional dividends, it is still possible to lose. If you restrict options trading to safe strategies such as covered calls, it works out most of the time but not every time. In the alternative, if you simply stay out of the markets, inflation eventually erodes the value of your capital.

The contingent options plan described in this book methodically builds an explanation of the system, beginning with an exploration of chart-based trade timing, followed by an examination of proximity and risk. It is disturbing that these two topics—chart reading and the nature of risk—are too often excluded from publication about options trading. Focus on the more immediate details of how to structure a trade is important to develop an understanding of a strategy, but even before selecting a favorite trade, you must understand risk;

and for that, observing proximity between the option and the underlying price is essential.

The next topics in the book are stock selection through fundamental analysis and timing of trades with exceptionally effective technical signals. These are the core of stock selection that leads to development of risk hedges with exceptional effectiveness. Too often, "hedging" is viewed as a method for eliminating risk on high-risk stocks. As an alternative, it makes more sense to first identify and buy low-risk stocks and then hedge market risk.

The next topic addressed is elimination of long-term market risk. Every investor who owns stock worries constantly about decline in a stock's price. The paper losses suffered as a result can lead to long-term realized losses, but this is not inevitable. The LEAPS put, bought as an insurance put, eliminates all market risk. In the traditional description of the insurance put, the risk cap occurs at the net of stock purchase price minus the cost of buying the put. In the risk hedge described in this book, the cost of the put is eliminated through a series of offsetting installment sales.

Like the zero-cost insurance put, the zero-cost LEAPS call freezes the price at the strike for future purchase. For example, you want to buy 100 shares of stock at today's price and you are concerned that if the price continues moving upward, you will lose the opportunity. At the same time, you are concerned that the price could reverse and fall. The contingent purchase of a LEAPS call solves both problems while also set to end up with a zero basis.

The idea of paying for long LEAPS options by selling short options concerns many traders. Yes, there are risks. But these risks are manageable and can be reduced through selection of strikes and timing of expiration; through observation of proximity and current price in relation to the overall trading range; and by recognition of reversal or continuation signals and strong confirmation.

In evaluating the use of short options, you also can expand beyond the basic strategy by using combinations. These change the risk profile for the entire position and can enrich the overall experience. One aspect to this plan that is easily overlooked is the long side flexibility. When the LEAPS option becomes profitable, it can be closed and replaced with a new installment strategy. You are not committed to seeing the strategy through to the expiration of the long option many months in the future.

The decision to expand into a combination hedge or to keep the strategy limited to short options depends on the current volatility in the underlying stock, and opens the possibility of using more than one method to pay for the LEAPS option.

The entire strategy can also be expanded in many ways. These are examined and described in detail. The selection of a strategy or a combination should also rely on the current volatility and momentum of the underlying, proximity of price to the trading range, and potential of one or more option contracts to perform well as a swing trade.

The strategic profits of installment ideas are only one side of the equation. Equally challenging is the management of losses when they occur. Sharp movement in the overall market does not mean a strategy fails; it does demand a thorough and sensible defensive plan. In addition to how a volatile market can be managed, you need to identify recovery strategies and be prepared to put them into effect. Most options traders recognize that the market is more complex than buying and selling, or than profits and losses. Hedging involves not only reduction of market risk, but recovery when losses occur despite your best efforts.

Options hedging is the most flexible method for accomplishing these goals. The installment option enables you to combine the need for long-term portfolio risk management, with the equally important desire to generate short-term profits.

Spring Hill, TN, USA   Michael C. Thomsett

Contents

1	**Chart-Based Trade Timing**	1
	The Key to Profitable Trades	2
	Advantageous Price Levels	4
	Price Patterns	6
	Candlesticks (Eastern)	8
	Western Price Indicators	10
	Non-price Signals	11
	Strong Fundamental Trends	12
2	**Proximity and Risk**	15
	Proximity and Moneyness	17
	Proximity to Expiration	18
	Proximity of Price to Resistance or Support	19
	Strongest Reversal Proximity	22
	Proximity in Consolidation Trends	24
	Risks in Every Strategy	26
	Collateral Requirements	27
	Options and Market Risk	28
3	**Picking the Right Stock**	31
	Fundamental Risk	32
	The Effect of Fundamental Trends on Options Risk	33
	Contingent Purchase and Stock Selection	35
	Contingent Sales as Risk Hedges of Stock	37

	Dividend Yield and Trends	39
	Debt to Total Capitalization Ratio and Trend	40
	P/E Annual Ranges	44
	Revenue and Earnings Trends	45
4	**Timing with Well-Selected Technical Signals**	**49**
	Entry and Exit Timing	50
	Resistance and Support	52
	Bollinger Bands	53
	T-Line	54
	Gaps and Tops or Bottoms	56
	Rounded Tops or Bottoms and Island Reversals	57
	Candlestick Reversal	59
	Candlestick Continuation	60
	Volume Indicators	61
	Momentum Oscillators	62
	Moving Averages	64
5	**Long-Term Market Risk Elimination**	**67**
	The Nature of Underlying Risk	68
	The Risk Hedge with Long Puts	71
	The Trade: Long-Term Long Put and Short-Term Short Positions	72
	Calculating the Point of Risk Elimination	75
	Possible Outcomes	77
6	**Long-Term Contingent Purchase**	**81**
	Locking in the Future Price	81
	The Risk Hedge for Future Purchase	84
	Calculating the Point of Risk Elimination	86
	Possible Outcomes	88
7	**Short Options and Levels of Risk**	**93**
	Unavoidable Risks	93
	Covered Calls for Risk Reduction	98
	Uncovered Puts for the Same Risk Profile	100
	Uncovered Calls and Varying Risk Levels	101
	Picking Calls or Puts Based on Price Proximity	102
	Exploiting Time Decay	104

8	**Alternative Offsets Beyond Short Calls or Short Puts**	107
	Synthetic Stock	107
	Vertical and Diagonal Spreads	111
	Straddles and Strangles	115
	Iron Butterfly	118
	Closing the Long-Term Option at a Profit	120
9	**Combining the Short Offset Alternatives**	123
	Current Price Proximity	123
	Historical Volatility	128
	Combining the Alternatives	130
	Multiple Increments and Combinations	136
10	**Expanding the Strategies**	139
	Rolling Techniques	140
	Long Collars	141
	Long-Term Long Straddles and Strangles	144
	Short-Term Short Straddles, Strangles and Spreads	147
	Covered Straddles and Strangles	148
	Straps and Strips	150
	Multiple Option Contracts	153
11	**Managing Potential Losses**	155
	Short Positions at Risk	156
	The Advantage of Time Decay	158
	Reducing Risk Exposure: Moneyness and Timing	159
	Avoiding Ex-dividend Periods	160
	Avoiding Earnings Week	161
	Short-Term Expiration Advantages	165
12	**Recovery Strategies**	167
	Protective and Responsive Loss Offsets	168
	Selective Rolling	169
	Closing and Taking Losses	171
	Entering New Positions with Higher Risks	172
	Expanding Exposed Spread Positions	172

13 The Flexibility of Options Hedging — 175
The Hedging and Leverage Advantage — 175
Installment Variations Based on Changing Conditions — 177
Adjusting to Sudden Price Movement — 178
Reducing Risks with Long-Term Hedging — 180

Bibliography — 183

Index — 187

List of Figures

Fig. 1.1	Reversal signals and confirmation	5
Fig. 1.2	Candidate for installment call	7
Fig. 1.3	Candidate for installment put	8
Fig. 1.4	The Japanese candlestick	9
Fig. 2.1	Resistance and support	21
Fig. 2.2	Dynamic resistance and support	21
Fig. 2.3	Consolidation trend	25
Fig. 2.4	Consolidation trend with breakout	25
Fig. 3.1	Sears Holding stock chart, one year	42
Fig. 4.1	Resistance and support	52
Fig. 4.2	Bollinger Bands	54
Fig. 4.3	Bollinger Bands and the t-line	55
Fig. 4.4	Gaps and tops or bottoms	57
Fig. 4.5	Rounded tops	58
Fig. 4.6	Rounded bottoms	58
Fig. 4.7	Island reversals	59
Fig. 4.8	Candlestick reversal signals	60
Fig. 4.9	Candlestick continuation signals	61
Fig. 4.10	Volume spike	62
Fig. 4.11	Relative strength index (RSI)	63
Fig. 4.12	Moving averages	64
Fig. 6.1	Three-year price charts, declining and advancing prices	83
Fig. 6.2	Outcomes of the installment purchase	85
Fig. 6.3	Lockheed Martin	90
Fig. 6.4	Netflix	91
Fig. 7.1	Price above three standard deviation upper Bollinger Band	97
Fig. 8.1	Chipotle (CMG)	112
Fig. 8.2	Covered straddle	116

Fig. 8.3	Iron butterfly	119
Fig. 9.1	Proximity of strike to resistance or support	124
Fig. 9.2	Proximity of reversal signals to resistance or support	127
Fig. 9.3	Bollinger Bands and historical volatility	129
Fig. 9.4	Price spike	130
Fig. 9.5	Synthetic stock trades	135
Fig. 10.1	Long collar trade	142
Fig. 10.2	Setup for long-term straddle or strangle	144
Fig. 10.3	Chart for covered straddle or strangle	148
Fig. 10.4	Chart for strap or strip trade	150
Fig. 11.1	Positive earnings surprise	164
Fig. 13.1	Large price movement	179

List of Tables

Table 3.1	Dividend per share comparison	40
Table 3.2	Sears long-term debt trend	42
Table 3.3	Comparison, debt and dividend trends	43
Table 3.4	P/E ratio trend comparison	44
Table 3.5	Revenue and earnings comparisons	46
Table 5.1	Risk hedge, Verizon	74
Table 6.1	Ten-year comparison	82
Table 6.2	Installment purchase comparisons	84
Table 6.3	Contingent purchase plan, Lockheed Martin	90
Table 7.1	OTM options comparison	103
Table 7.2	Company comparison	103
Table 8.1	Target, synthetic long stock	108
Table 8.2	Target, synthetic short stock	109
Table 8.3	Option listings, Chipotle (CMG)	113
Table 8.4	Options listings, FedEx (FDX)	116
Table 8.5	Option listings, Tesla (TSLA)	119
Table 9.1	Two-direction hedge, Helmerich & Payne	131
Table 9.2	Synthetic stock trades	134

1

Chart-Based Trade Timing

Many papers and books have been published criticizing the use of technical indicators. These have cited the unreliability of past price behavior, and state preference for pricing models and options-based volatility analysis. One study concluded, for example, that

> high derivative rollers who use technical analysis and have speculation as their primary investment objective exhibit the same behavioral traits as investors who favor lottery stocks … technical analysis is associated with greater portfolio concentration, more turnover, less betting on trends, more options trading, a higher ratio of nonsystematic risk to total risk, lower gross and net returns, and lower risk-adjusted returns.[1]

This paper assumes that options traders relying on technical analysis are interested primarily in speculation. The premise in this book is that chart-based analysis and the use of technical signals is effective for *hedging* and not for speculation. Consequently, the assumptions in the cited paper might be true for speculative activity and not for hedging activity. It remains a primary point in using underlying technical analysis and charting, that relying on implied volatility (IV) to time options trades is a flawed method and tracking historical volatility (HV) yields a superior and more reliable result for trade timing.

> Conventional wisdom views derivatives markets as markets for risk transfer. According to this view, derivatives markets exist to facilitate the transfer of market risk from firms that wish to avoid such risks to others more willing or better suited to manage those risks. The important thing to note in this regard is that derivatives

markets do not create new risks—they just facilitate risk management. Viewed from this perspective, the rapid growth of derivatives markets in recent years simply reflects advances in the technology of risk management.[2]

This observation raises an issue regarding the hedging attributes of options, as related to an equity portfolio. Not only is hedging a more rational utility of options, it also has progressed as a mechanism for risk management based on the cited advances in technology. Anyone who studies underlying security charts and analyzes price trends with technical indicators is aware of these advances. It makes use of technical analysis of the underlying both practical and effective for hedging activities.

In comparison, there are two flaws in relying on options-specific signals. First, they are artificial and based on unreliable estimates. Second, options value is derived from volatility and price movement in the underlying. This is why options are also termed *derivatives*. Their value is not independent, and contrary to popular belief, options volatility does *not* lead price of the underlying. So many myths permeate the options world, and the many "urban legends" about how option and underlying behavior are created only make it more difficult to definitively appreciate how this industry works.

When traders abandon the belief in IV and similar analyses favored by the academic world but rarely by the real-world trader, they can turn to charts to gain a sense of how price behavior and related indicators reveal what is likely to occur in options value in the future.

The Key to Profitable Trades

Chartists do not subscribe to a belief that past price trends are reliable to predict the future. They do acknowledge that the pattern and momentum of current price provide indications of what is *likely* to happen next. The direction of short-term and long-term trends, rate of movement, interim volatility (e.g. characterized by seesaw price patterns or repetitive gaps) and other technical signals reveal the level of market risk to a stock and its options.

It is not accurate to dismiss charting and observation of past price patterns as the sole theory behind technical analysis. Considering the role of options may add to price discovery (determination of an accurate current price of a security) for the underlying, improving both selection of equities and timing of trades:

Empirical evidence suggests that the presence of listed options is associated with higher market quality in the market for the underlying asset. A plausible explanation for this effect is that the presence of a correlated asset permits the sharing of effective price discovery across markets: if market makers in the stock learn from transactions in the option they can set more accurate prices.[3]

The implication of this evidence is profound. It indicates that technical analysis should not be viewed as an isolated system for "guessing" future price movement based on past price movement. Rather, technical analysis appears to serve a purpose in the timing of stock trades, and that options play a role in bringing greater order to equity markets.

Price behavior is complex and results from many influences beyond the limited forces of supply and demand. The movement is viewed in charts of an underlying security and volatility itself reflects actual recent price activity. This means that the HV of the security indicates the best (and worst) timing for options trading. The academic focus on IV and models such as the Black-Scholes pricing model is meant to provide a sense of reliability to options pricing, when in fact traders live with uncertainty. Even with the best signals and formulas, IV is an estimate based on assumptions with no basis in fact. Its calculation and outcome rely on the use of an assumed risk-free interest rate. According to NASDAQ, this rate "describes return available to an investor in a security somehow guaranteed to produce that return."[4]

The rate used usually is a US Treasury rate or a similar rate considered to provide ironclad safety (risk-free), although such a rate cannot exist beyond the realm of theory. However, IV—because it is based on assumptions and is intended to forecast future volatility—is not a reliable estimate of coming option price levels. It is a more rational measure of options pricing in relation to its value in comparison to other options with identical or similar terms.

The rational conclusion is that calculating IV does not provide a reliable, consistent method for profitable trades or for their entry or exit timing. For this, a practical reliance on technical indicators does provide worthwhile data. However, you set up a more dependable system by first selecting companies based on fundamental trends over many years, as a means for narrowing the field of issues on which you will trade options.

The trends discovered in dividends, price/earnings (P/E) ratio annual range, revenues and earnings and debt capitalization are a short list of fundamental trends, but they clearly define how well management controls its fundamental volatility. This is a tendency for financial outcomes to perform in a reliable manner, or to be inconsistent from year to year. Fundamental volatility consistently creates technical volatility in the stock price. A low-volatile fundamental status translates to low-volatility technical status, and high fundamental volatility sets up high technical volatility. The lag time between fundamental and technical outcomes is not consistent, but over many years the relationship clearly can be observed.

Even with the problem of inconsistent lag in the impact of fundamental on technical results, using both makes the most sense. Fundamental analysis yields better long-term results in equity selection, but for options trading, fundamentals do not always impact timing as quickly as technical signals:

> [S]tock performance results relying on the fundamental analysis have higher success rate than the models relying on technical analysis data … the variable set produced by means of the technical and the fundamental analyses data [combined] … over performed the averages of separate models based on the fundamental and the technical analyses.[5]

Once fundamental value has been established, the next step is to analyze the stock of a company on a technical basis. How volatile is the stock price? The HV is based on recent trading range and momentum in the stock price, and as volatility is seen to increase or decrease, you gain a sense of market risk. This in turn is used to decide whether to trade options, and whether to focus on long positions (at times of low HV) or short options (at times of high HV).

Advantageous Price Levels

The status of HV can be thought of as identifying when underlying price levels are advantage for options trading. Options trades should be made according to the price levels of the underlying in relation to the overall trading range. For example, a short call is most advantageous when entered with the underlying price near the top of the trading range. If the price gaps through the trading range, the advantage is at its greatest.

A short put is most advantageous at the opposite level of the trading range. When the underlying price is at a low, timing is ideal for a short put. If price has gapped below support, timing is optimal.

For long options, the opposite proximity is applied. Long calls are best entered when price is at its support level; if price has gapped below support, timing is best. For long puts, the same is true if the underlying price is at resistance. If it has gapped above resistance, the long put is most likely to perform well.

In all these conditions, it is possible that the price movement or breakout is the first signal of a new trend. In those cases, opening an option based on the assumption that price is most likely to retreat into range would be a mistake.

You need to look for price and other signals (volume, momentum, moving average) to identify reversal signals and confirmation before entering a trade. If these signals are not located, a trade should not be made.

If the search for signals results in a continuation indicator and confirmation, it predicts that the price direction will continue. As a result, assuming price reversal would be ill advised. You want to find clear and strong signals for the timing of trades based on advantageous price levels, and that assumes that reversal is the next step.

For example, in Fig. 1.1, a lengthy bullish trend was accompanied by a warning indicator in relative strength index (RSI), a momentum oscillator. This index resided in the "overbought" level above 70 for nearly two months, before price reversed and declined.

When the price fell in early February, it moved below the lower Bollinger Band, and this always leads to a return into range. The move below the lower band was the first signal of a coming bullish reversal. Confirming this were two candlestick signals. First was the highlighted piercing lines and second was the bullish harami. These signals were accompanied by a series of volume spikes.

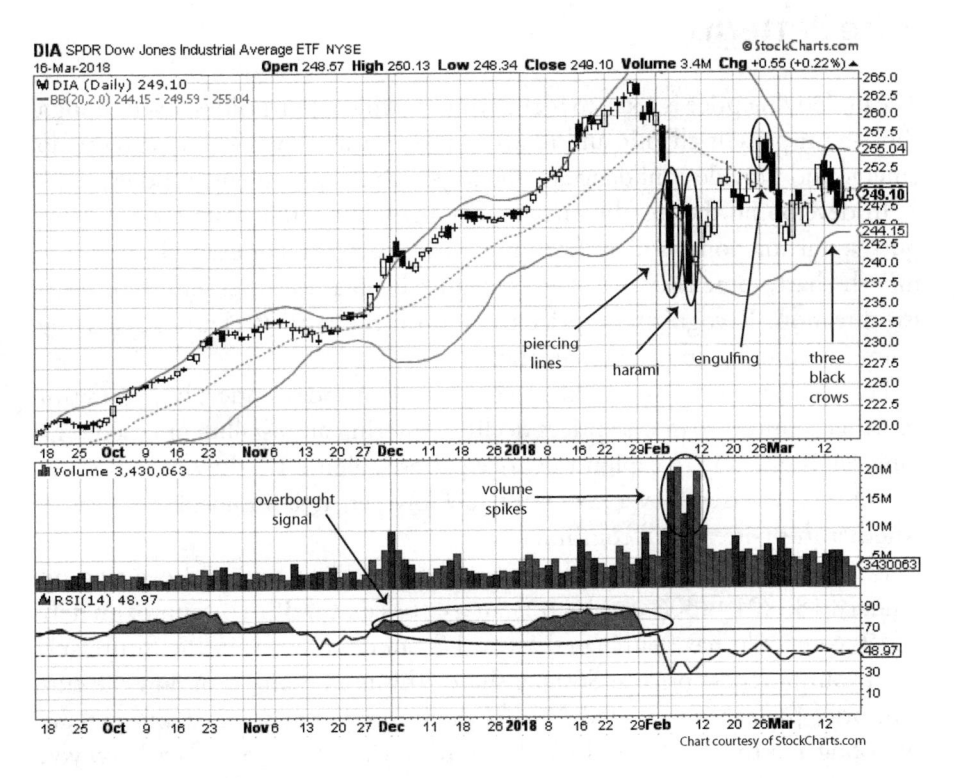

Fig. 1.1 Reversal signals and confirmation

All these signals—price moving below lower band, two candlestick signals and the set of volume spikes—predicted a reversal and price movement to the upside. The resulting move did occur, culminating in a bearish candlestick, the engulfing pattern. The bearish indicator was confirmed by another candlestick signal, three black crows.

This example of signals of many types (Bollinger Bands, which is a moving average (MA) with probability ranges; volume; momentum and price signals) reveals that the timing of options trades can be made skillfully and based on well-confirmed reversal signals. If you traded this issue, identifying tops and bottoms was not difficult, and the price pattern in relation to resistance and support aided in identifying the tops and bottoms. The use of Bollinger Bands to set up a dynamic version of these trading range borders is a method for determining how a trading range evolves in a period of strong trends. For traders using signals like this, identifying opportunities to open and trade installment-based options becomes much easier than the more common practice of selection based largely on guesswork or use of signals without confirmation.

Price Patterns

The underlying price is a key to identifying trading opportunities. Even though short-term price is chaotic and tends to move erratically, specific patterns do emerge and provide confidence to you as you time options entry and exit.

In developing the installment strategy involving either long-term calls or puts, a starting point is identification of price patterns. For example, on a six-month chart, some issues display a recognizable bias in either bullish or bearish direction. Recognizing a price pattern on the current chart is a starting point for entering an installment trade.

For example, if you would like to buy shares at today's price, but you want to hedge a purchase in case prices decline, entering an installment based on a long call is one way to exploit the price pattern. Figure 1.2 shows a pattern of a bullish price trend over six months. However, it is impossible to know whether this pattern will continue.

In this situation, buying a LEAPS call at a strike of 60 and expiring on January 18, 2019 (306 days), costs an ask price of 4.35. For approximately $440, you could have purchased a LEAPS call ten months in the future and fixed your purchase price at $60 per share. This is an example of how the current price pattern is exploited. You fix the future purchase price, but you are not obligated to buy shares. In addition to buying shares 306 days later, you could also sell the call before expiration and take profits if the stock price

Fig. 1.2 Candidate for installment call

moved higher. If the stock price was below the strike of 60, you do not have to take any action, and if the $440 call was paid for in the interim, market risk was eliminated.

This is all based on observation of the current price pattern. This company's stock was on the rise over the past six months and you could easily estimate that this trend will continue (but it might not). The LEAPS call installment freezes the price but eliminates the market risk of buying shares today.

Another example: you own shares in a company and you expect the price to rise in the future. But you are also concerned that recent price patterns of a bearish nature could continue. Do you cut your losses and sell shares? Or do you freeze market risk with a LEAPS put? The price pattern is of great concern, but that concern can be erased with a well-timed LEAPS put purchase, as shown in Fig. 1.3.

The LEAPS 87.50 put expiring on January 18, 2019 (306 days), had an ask price of 6.45. This could be purchased for approximately $650 when trading fees are added. The put is paid for with a series of short-term option positions over the ten-month period. The installment call froze the price for future purchase; the installment put eliminates market risk below the strike, notably since the net cost of the long put is reduced to zero over time, as short options are sold. At any time before expiration, if the underlying price is below the 87.50 strike, the put can be exercised, and shares sold at that fixed strike; or the put can be sold, and profits taken. If the price of stock is higher than the put's strike, no action needs to be taken, and the put expires worthless.

Fig. 1.3 Candidate for installment put

These are examples of how price patterns indicate the timing for either an installment call or an installment put. Other options strategies, either speculative swing trades or hedges to protect equity positions, are also based on price patterns and proximity between price and the trading range.

Candlesticks (Eastern)

Price patterns reveal the current trend, and reversal or continuation is indicated in price signals. Among the most effective of these are Japanese candlesticks, also called "Eastern" technical signals. Some traders use candlestick charts regularly but might not necessarily understand the power and effectiveness of candlestick signals.

Any technical system will involve an attempt to add predictive value to the current trend, which itself may be elusive:

> The central objective is to determine whether the candlestick reversal patterns have any predictive value. The reversal patterns are expected to be valid only when prices are in the appropriate trend. Formulating a suitable mathematical definition of trend is a delicate issue, since those given by technical analysts often make use of 'channels' that would be highly parametric in nature and subject to interpretation.[6]

The challenge of identifying the trend is considerable, and in this regard, candlesticks are useful in articulating whether a trend does exist or simply is a random movement of price. Reversal and continuation signals vary in strength, so an especially strong signal adds confidence that a trend is underway.

Candlesticks often are viewed in terms of price rather than price *and* trend. One session's candlestick is information, but a range of consecutive candlesticks reveals strength or weakness of price, the direction of movement, volatility within each session and longevity of the trend.

The Japanese candlestick has become the default format for modern charting, replacing the previously used OHLC (open, high, low, close) or point and figure chart. Before the Internet, construction of a candlestick chart would have been time-consuming and demanding a lot of research; today, the formulation is automated and easily available on many free online charting services. These include stockcharts.com, which is used on all the stock charts in this book.

Figure 1.4 demonstrates what the candlestick reveals. A white or clear candlestick occurs when price moves upward in a session, and a black candlestick is used for downward-moving days. Some services used green and red candlesticks in place of white and black, but this is confusing. Many of the candlestick patterns include the word "white" or "black" as part of a descriptive name.

The candlestick also identifies the day's trading range from open to close, represented by a rectangle (called the "real body"). A white candlestick opens at the bottom and closes at the top, and a black candlestick opens at the top and closes at the bottom. This enables immediate recognition of the direction of movement as well as the extent. A long rectangle means many points moved

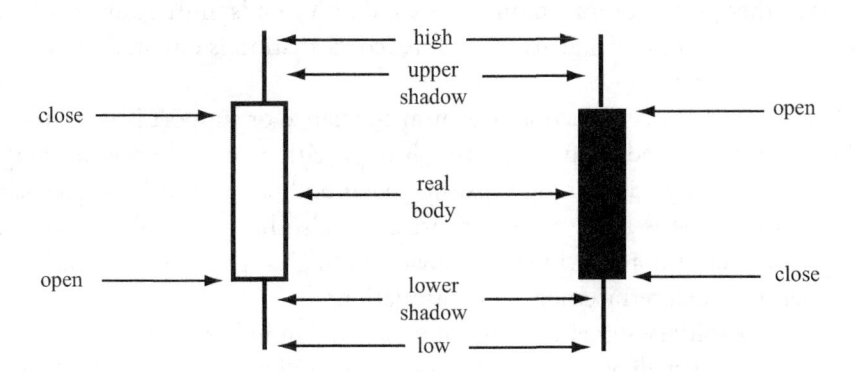

Fig. 1.4 The Japanese candlestick

from open to close; a narrow-range candlestick means price did not change from opening to closing price (the extreme would be opening and closing at the same price with the rectangle replaced by a horizontal line, and the day is termed a *doji*).

The vertical lines extending above and below the real body are called shadows, or wicks. These represent the extent of trading above and below the opening and closing prices. Long shadows reveal weakness among buyers (the upper shadow) or seller (the lower shadow). Price moved to the extent of the shadow but could not be sustained at those levels.

The candlestick provides information about price as well as the price trend. Comparing candlestick activity to an established resistance and support level also helps in identifying a likely breakout above or below price, or a retreat into range. This adds to the information available about timing of trades. In the installment strategy, maximizing the timing of a short trade is essential to achieve the goal, while is to pay for the LEAPS call or put. The signals generated by candlesticks are numerous, and many are exceptionally reliable for swing trading and for the timing of short options. Even so, the reliability of candlestick signals varies, so that confirmation is always a requirement beyond the initial signal.

Western Price Indicators

Although modern charting is based on candlesticks rather than on old-style OHLC and other systems, traditional Western price indicators continue to offer value in timing of trades. The chartist who relies on Western signals among other price, volume, momentum and MA trends must be aware of the variation in strength of signals. Therefore, confirmation is essential upon recognizing any signal.

For example, price behavior at or near resistance or support is very strong when also confirmed. If price moves through either of these trading range borders, especially with strong gaps, the likelihood of a retreat into establishing trading range is high. However, price can also break out of the existing range and establish a new higher or lower trading range. How do you know whether to expect retracement or continuation?

Because a solitary signal does not provide enough information to know the answer, you must depend on a second signal indicating reversal back into range *or* continuation to new higher or lower trading ranges. Activity near or through resistance and support is where most reversals occur, but this does not preclude the possibility of continuation.

Beyond the reliability of strong signals and confirmation in close proximity to resistance and support, other technical signals in dozens of configurations can initiate analysis to determine what is likely to occur next. Signals like double tops or bottoms, rounded tops or bottoms, head and shoulders and island reversals are all examples of strong reversal signals. However, by themselves, these signals do not provide enough information to act. You also need confirmation before entering a trade.

Some Western technical signals are weak or questionable and should not be used with high confidence. Examples include the range of signals known as wedges and triangles. A rising wedge consists of both resistance and support moving upward, but also moving closer together. As the two lines converge, a bearish reversal is signaled. A falling wedge is the opposite, two falling lines converging to set up a bullish reversal. The ascending triangle is very similar to the rising wedge, with the exception that the resistance level does not move up but remains at the same price level. It is a continuation signal, so as support rises close to resistance, a breakout is expected above the triangle's range. A declining triangle consists of level support and declining resistance, forecasting a bearish breakout.

The problem with these two sets of signals—wedges and triangles—is that they are similar in their formation, but they have opposite interpretations. Depending on where you draw the lines, a formation can be interpreted as either a wedge or a triangle. But is the indication a reversal or continuation? The uncertainty draws into question the value of both sets of signals.

This example makes the point that all forms of signaling can be interpreted to mean different "likely" forecasts. The need for confirmation of reversal or continuation signals is based on the point that no signal is reliable all the time, and in some cases (such as wedges and triangles) the next step in price behavior is a matter of opinion.

Non-price Signals

Beyond price signals, volume also gives traders numerous indicators. Under the Dow Theory of technical analysis, volume leads price; you often see volume signals in advance of price reaction.

The easiest volume signal to observe is the spike. When the level of volume is far greater on one session (or two consecutive sessions) than the average, it often means a big price adjustment is underway. This can precede the move in price, but more often, it occurs as price gaps higher or lower in the same session. The sudden keen interest in the security often results from earning surprises, acquisitions, changes in management or new product lines. For the swing trader, the volume spike is short-term confirmation of price behavior, but after the spike, price often returns to previous levels. The volume spike does not confirm a new price trend, but it does confirm the strength of a move, whether temporary or permanent.

Many other volume indicators are popularly used in chart analysis and are of varying reliability. As with all non-price signals, volume indicators should be used as confirmation rather than as leading signals.

Momentum refers to the strength and speed of price movement, and oscillators measure these tendencies. However, oscillators do not measure the direction of price movement. They do indicate when the underlying security is overbought or oversold, however. As a confirmation indicator, the oscillator helps you to identify the intensity of a current trend, whether moving upward or downward. Among the most popular and easily understood of momentum oscillators is the RSI, which tracks price movement over an average of 14 sessions. This is expressed on a scale between 0 and 100. When the index value rises above 70, it indicates that the stock is overbought; when it declines below 30, it indicates that the stock is oversold. Because RSI, like all oscillators, is a lagging indicator, it should not be used by itself. It is a strong confirmation signal, however, when other signals indicate a coming reversal.

Oscillators combine various forms of price-based MAs to develop index values and trends. A more basic form of analysis is the MA itself, to test price but not momentum. Chartists use MAs in combination. For example, overlaying price with a 50-session and a 200-session MA at the same time. The shorter term MA is more reactive to price changes, so as the two averages converge or diverge, or as price crossed above or below one of the MA lines, traders interpret the change as a forecast of what is likely to occur next.

A problem with relying on MA trends is in the nature of the average itself. It is a lagging indicator, the result of what happened in the past rather than predicting the future. The MA trends are useful in confirming what other signals predict, but MA does not lead price or forecast the next direction; it is only a summary of past price trends.

Strong Fundamental Trends

Options traders often reply on IV, which is the estimate of future volatility in the option. This analysis is based on estimated values but not solely on price behavior in the underlying security. The use of estimates for risk-free interest (a theoretical value only) makes IV questionable. Because options prices are derived from behavior and volatility in the underlying security (thus the term "derivative"), greater value can be drawn from fundamental trends, especially in the degree to which these trends affect price behavior in the underlying.

A much more reliable test is HV, the trend of stock prices. Because this is based on actual price movement, it is more precise than the entirely unrelated IV. While IV attempts to estimate future price movement in the option (which relies on estimates), HV can be used to spot the ebb and flow of recent price. When HV is trending wider, the opportunity to profit from selling options increases; when it begins shrinking, option prices will also decline and the opportunity to profit from buying options increases.

The previously introduced Bollinger Bands allows you to see HV on the price chart. This indicator consists of three bands. The middle band is a 20-session simple MA of price. The upper and lower bands are each two standard deviations removed from the middle band (as a result, they are always the same distance above and below). Standard deviation is a statistical calculation based on the averaging of the square root of variances. This is a powerful analytical tool because it is unusual for price to move above or below the outer bands; when price does go outside of the Bollinger bandwidth, it represents an exceptional reversal signal.

By tracking HV based on Bollinger Bands, you develop a starting point for technical analysis. Dozens of additional signals, used together to spot reversal and to confirm it, give you a powerful set of signals for timing of options trades. Skillful use of technical signals for price, volume, momentum and MAs increases confidence about what is taking place in the price trend of the underlying. As a direct result, your timing for entry and exit of options trades is vastly improved.

Using the underlying security's price chart to spot technical signals is the best method for (a) spotting likely price trends, (b) determining whether trends are likely to continue, stop or reverse and (c) timing option entry and exit to exploit the moves anticipated by this range of signals. Without the chart, it would be difficult, if not impossible, to estimate the trend and price strength or weakness. The underlying security's chart should serve as the guiding visual tool for developing an options program.

As part of that program, timing for the two types of installment strategies can be made based on information rather than on instinct or emotion. A trader who wants to freeze today's price per share to buy later (as much as two years or more in the future) may buy a LEAPS call and pay for it with weekly short options. A trader who owns shares and wants to eliminate all market risk can create a no-cost hedge using a LEAPS put. Both strategies rely on your analysis of the underlying chart and what it reveals.

As the next chapter explains, the skill to time entry and exit depends on analysis of proximity—between price and strike, and between price and the trading range. Proximity often is overlooked or ignored in options literature and replaced with the vague estimates of IV. Ignoring proximity is a mistake, for at least one reason: it tells the whole story of timing for options trades.

Notes

1. Hoffmann, A. & Shefrin, H. (2014). Technical analysis and individual investors. *Journal of Economic Behavior & Organization* 107, pp. 487–511.
2. Kuprianov, A. (Fall 1995). Derivatives debacle. *Economic Quarterly*, Vol. 81, Issue 4.
3. Jong, C., Koedijk, K. & Schnitzlein, C. (July 2006). Stock market quality in the presence of a traded option. *The Journal of Business*, Vol. 79, No. 4, pp. 2243–2274.
4. https://www.nasdaq.com/investing/glossary/r/risk-free-interest-rate, retrieved March 19, 2018.
5. Emir, S.; Dinçer, H.; & Timor, M. (August 2012). A stock selection model based on fundamental and technical analysis variables by using artificial neural networks and support vector machines. *Review of Economics & Finance*, Vol. 2, pp. 106–122.
6. Caginalp, G. & Laurent, H. (February 1998). The predictive power of price patterns. *Applied Mathematical Finance*, Vol. 5, Issue 3–4, pp. 181–205.

2

Proximity and Risk

The concept of *proximity* is at the core of the installment strategy. In selecting a LEAPS call as part of a long-term purchase strategy, you need to track the recent price trend in the underlying and to develop a sense of the longer term trend itself. A short-term reaction or swing trend does not tell the entire story. A review of at least 6–12 months of price movement is required to estimate a likely longer term estimate of price activity.

An evaluation of risk for all options strategies should not ignore the reality: there are no absolute guarantees (in options or anywhere else) that a position will be profitable. Market does not go away, but it can be hedged. You must adopt a realistic view of risk and avoid what many traders do, which is to attempt to escape risk altogether. Experience and knowledge do not improve your chances of escaping risk; it is a reality:

> Even if the trader has correctly estimated current market conditions, it's possible that over time conditions will change in a way that will adversely affect the value of his option position. Because of the many forces affecting an option's value, price can change in ways which may surprise even the most experienced trader.[1]

Risk, even though unavoidable, is *manageable* with the risk hedge. The ability to freeze today's price for potential future profit, or to eliminate all market risk on a currently held equity position, provides powerful hedging not available without an installment strategy. In selecting a LEAPS put to eliminate all market risk below a selected strike, the proximity of that strike to the initial purchase price determines whether the risk truly can be eliminated. If a strike is selected below the initial purchase price, the risk hedge will eliminate only part of the risk. A strike selected at or above initial cost not only eliminates market risk below the strike but also ensures that there are no losses based on initial price paid for shares.

The ability to hedge varies not only by the nature of a position and the overall market, but also by the experience and knowledge of an individual trader or investor. Outcomes in one study concluded that price behavior of a selected position varied based on whether the individual had considerable experience about the markets (an "informed investor") or was a relative novice:

> Motivated by this understanding and the inconsistent results in the previous literature, we hypothesize that the price effects and information roles of trade duration can differ depending on the traits and proportions of investors, or more specifically, the different compositions of informed and uninformed investors participating in the market.[2]

This observation describes the nature of risk itself. A risk hedge of any nature is not applicable universally to all traders. The experience levels count. An informed investor will exert skill in the timing and selection of strategies, so that risk hedging is not as critical to success as it would be for a novice. This further points out the nature of options trading in a broader sense: an uninformed investor is at greater risk than an informed investor, simply due to the lack of experience in timing and selection of trades. The information level between informed and uninformed investors is one of many factors to consider before entering trades or attempting to hedge risk. A wise but uninformed investor would avoid risky situations requiring a risk hedge, and an informed investor is more likely to apply risk hedging to mitigate risk while also understanding that some risks do not require hedging. Timing of expiration, proximity and moneyness of the option, and volatility of the underlying security all play a role in the evaluation and analysis of risk.

However, it is an error to assume that uninformed investors recognize their own limitations. One form of risk is among uninformed investors who may create irrational levels of trading beyond rational justification. The theory of trading "emphasizes the distinction between informed and uninformed agents, trading itself is driven by agents with convictions, whether or not they possess valid information." Consequently,

> one of the great puzzles of finance is the sheer volume of trading, which seems far in excess of what could reasonably be anticipated based on the arrival of new private information. Presumably, some of this seemingly excessive trading is among agents who are not informed at all, but simply believe they are.[3]

The variable of experience and knowledge is as crucial to the success of a risk hedge as the selection of a strategy. The two aspects—strategy selection and knowledge—work together, and no formula of hedging can counter a lack of experience and knowledge among traders.

Proximity and Moneyness

A great deal of literature in the options market has been focused on comparisons between in the money (ITM), out of the money (OTM) and at the money (ATM) options. These levels of moneyness react to price movement in different ways. Mathematical formulas based on delta and gamma further attempt to quantify moneyness and price behavior. Delta measures the impact on options of price movement in the underlying, and understandably, delta is going to be different for variations in the moneyness of the option. Gamma measures the rate of change in delta. These formulations are worthwhile for articulating the importance of moneyness.

Developing options based on delta or gamma may introduce risks not anticipated in the options literature, and often realized in disappointing performance. Delta hedging (e.g. long call versus shorted stock) is generally believed to eliminate all market risks, but the complexity of the option side in this hedge often will reduce the risk hedge. Complexity itself may be at fault. One study observed that

> the exotic feature of the option under consideration has a great impact on the relative performance of different option-pricing models. In addition, for any given model, the more "exotic" the option, the poorer the hedging effectiveness.[4]

This indicates that hedging with delta or gamma might not be most effectively used to create hedging strategies. They are useful in identifying the levels of volatility and relative movement in the option versus the underlying. However, beyond that, it is possible to misread how delta and gamma create opportunities or risks. Quantifying moneyness should not need to rely on calculating delta or gamma as a starting point.

The moneyness of the option is easily observed and obvious even without calculating delta and gamma. To the academic world of options analysis, this claim may be shocking; but it is true. If you, as an options trader, understand that moneyness affects the reaction of option value to underlying price movement, there should be no surprises.

It has been observed and documented that ITM options are most likely to experience the closest possible one-to-one changes in option and the underlying. Intrinsic value tracks the underlying point for point, leaving the only variables (1) implied volatility premium in the option and (2) time to expiration. An ATM option also responds closely to movement in the underlying. However, movement of ATM to ITM will be more responsive than OTM, if only because intrinsic value is in play.

Options that are OTM are the least likely to track corresponding movement in the underlying. The further the OTM option is from current underlying price, the less responsive it will be. Expiration timing also affects OTM pricing. Deep OTM options are likely to display little or no movement, especially when expiration is farther away.

Proximity to Expiration

A related form of proximity also affected by moneyness is the time to expiration. The closer the expiration date, the more rapidly time decay occurs. As a result, the expiration proximity has a direct relationship to moneyness, and behaves in a predictable manner. For those opening long options positions, rapid time decay is a problem, but longer term options react less and cost more.

Which matter more, time or price? They work together, of course. However, in seeking bargains, traders might end up placing more importance on price and less on time:

> Price change often becomes the overriding consideration when dealing in securities. Many people talk in terms of making a certain percent on an investment, but rarely relate it to the time factor, failing to realize that rate of return is a function of both time and change.[5]

This comparison between price and time defines value. A 4 percent return on a one-month option is worth twice as much as a 4 percent return on a two-month option, when both returns are annualized:

$$4\% \div 1 \text{ month} * 12 \text{ months} = 48\%$$

$$4\% \div 2 \text{ months} * 12 \text{ months} = 24\%$$

This comparison of how time affects apparent return on an option trade is further influenced by proximity between current date and expiration. For traders opening short calls or puts, proximity to expiration is an advantage.

For example, writing a series of weekly options can be advantageous because time decay is rapid. The Friday before expiration is perhaps the best date to open a short option. Between Friday and Monday, three calendar days pass but only one trading day. As a result, approximately one-third of remaining time value evaporates between Friday and Monday before expiration. However, short options traders are correctly concerned about the risk of holding open positions between sessions, and especially over a weekend. If you can tolerate the risk of significant price movement over a weekend, this timing is the most advantageous for short positions.

This observation points to the advantage in an installment strategy. The goal is to use short-term short positions to pay for the long-term LEAPS option. A series of positions opened on the Friday before expiration and closed at some point between Monday and expiration Friday will be most likely to accomplish the goal of the installment strategy.

Proximity of Price to Resistance or Support

Timing of all trades often is done without regard to the current proximity of price to the borders of the trading range, resistance and support.

Resistance is the top price the underlying reaches under prevailing conditions. As price rises, resistance is the likely price point at which price will reverse and move back into mid-range. If price moves through resistance, especially with a gap, it is even more likely to reverse. However, a breakout above resistance also can mark the beginning of a new trend, culminating in a newly established trading range. In some cases, previous resistance flips to become the new support in the higher trading range.

Support is found at the bottom of the trading range. As price declines to support, it is likely to reverse and head back into mid-range. When price declines below support, it might strengthen the likelihood of reversal, or it might be the beginning of a new, lower trading range. Previous support might flip to become new resistance in this lower range.

Proximity of these crucial price levels is at the core of a timing strategy. If price remains within the existing trading range, the timing of long puts (or short calls) is maximized at or through the resistance level. And the timing of long calls (or short puts) is maximized at or through support. This assumes that the timing of entering a trade occurs with three aspects present: (1) price at the trading range borders, (2) a reversal signal and (3) a second confirmation signal.

If all three of these aspects are not present, making a trade is ill-timed. The lack of a reversal signal might reveal the possibility of continuation. The move toward and through resistance or support can be identified as a breakout when three aspects are present. These are the same above, with one exception: instead of a reversal signal, you find a price continuation signal and confirmation.

The practice of technical analysis is relatively new in the markets. As recently as the 1960s, it was considered a novelty not used by very many traders. At that time, candlestick charts were virtually unknown, and this was not introduced in the Western world until Steve Nison discovered this ancient art: "In December 1989, I authored a two-page article on candle charts. This was the first information on the subject ever written by a non-Japanese."[6]

This period was also years before the Internet. Because of this, all forms of analysis were difficult to locate, especially timely analysis. In those pre-Internet times, traders paid thousands of dollars to subscribe to charting services, and the charts were sent by mail and were out of date by the time the trader received them.

The mysterious and often questionable practice of technical analysis was explained in a paper of the time:

> With a growing number of professionals seeking to find new ways of improving investment performance, it is, therefore, hardly surprising that, in the past few years, an ever-increasing number of analysts have turned their attention to technical analysis. It was barely a decade ago that the average portfolio manager, if he was aware of technical analysis at all, regarded it as some sort of black magic. Today, almost all professionals have at least a familiarity with the terminology and a good many make such analysis a major part of their decision-making process.[7]

The relatively new "black magic" of technical analysis remains controversial today, with many—especially in academia—considering it a worthless exercise. Proponents of the random walk hypothesis or efficient market hypothesis argue that price movement cannot be predicted accurately. Even so, evidence seems to indicate that using indicators such as resistance and support provides reliable predictive benefits.

For example, in Fig. 2.1, price is dynamic, first trending upward for four months and then downward for the last two. The consistent breadth of trading creates a channel, with resistance at the top and support at the bottom. This adds clear reliability to the prevailing trend, which continues until a reversal appears. In the middle of January, the strong bullish trend came to an abrupt halt and prices began moving sideways. This could have been interpreted as a warning that a reversal was about to occur.

Proximity and Risk   21

Fig. 2.1 Resistance and support

Fig. 2.2 Dynamic resistance and support

In this example using the traditional straight lines to mark resistance and support, the channels are easily observed. Because priced trends often are dynamic, an improved system of marking resistance and support is by overlaying Bollinger Bands. The previous chart is shown once again in Fig. 2.2, this time with the overlay to identify dynamic resistance and support.

The chart is significantly different with Bollinger Bands. It reveals instances when price moved above dynamic resistance or below dynamic support. The chart further reveals that these moves outside of the Bollinger bandwidth normally result in reversal. This may occur in a sideways price move (as in the moves above the upper band) or in a dramatic and swift reversal (as in the moves below the lower band). Over the entire period, the upper and lower bands mark the borders of the trading range. This is coordinated with the observation of historical volatility, also represented by bandwidth. As the distance between upper and lower bands increases, so does historical volatility; as it decreases, the opposite outcome occurs.

However, the validity of resistance and support as test points for reversal is not settled science, but a matter of opinion. To many market observers, the trading range does not provide strong evidence that reversal timing can be accurately timed:

> The reasoning which asserts the existence of support and resistance levels does not define the quantity of trading necessary to establish a level, or the length of time that it might last Further, it attributes a singular behavior to investors, and it tends to assume that market fluctuations will take place within a given range … Like the Dow Theory, support levels and resistance levels command little serious attention.[8]

This condemnation of support and resistance (which technicians tend to view as the organizing structure of analysis itself) is contrary to a widespread reliance on technical analysis. The author favors (in the same article) paying more attention to the odd-lot ratio and short interest, which are far more esoteric and uncertain than support and resistance. The ability to visualize the trading range of a stock through Bollinger Bands is indisputable and for timing of trades, identification of reversal and tracking of momentum, the value of the trading range cannot be dismissed. The author raises interesting points in observing that investor behavior is not singular, and duration of a trading range is not indicated by these signals; but these are not indicated by any other signals either. Options traders must rely on a combination of indicators to time trades. This reliance includes analysis of moneyness, time to expiration and price.

It is all a matter of proximity. Price movement causes changes in historical volatility, and Bollinger bandwidth is a reliable and visual representation of this. When price is located at the top of the bandwidth, it is the correct proximity for short calls and long puts. When price is in proximity to the bottom of the bandwidth, it identifies timing for long calls or short puts.

Strongest Reversal Proximity

The proximity test is not limited to price itself. It also refers to patterns and to reversal signals.

These come in numerous shapes and sizes. Reversals limited to price (the most common) may take the shape of a candlestick signal that is confirmed. It may also take the shape of a traditional Western reversal; these include double tops or bottoms, head and shoulders, gaps, rounded tops or bottoms or island clusters.

The level of reliability in technical analysis, specifically in locating and acting on reversal signals, is not a fixed matter. It varies. The most significant factor influencing reliability is proximity of reversal signals—to resistance or support, and to moneyness as well:

> Technical Analysis does not provide us with definite answers as to this is the right or the wrong time to take an appropriate position into the market but surely it will act as a guide in improving trading capabilities to almost 80 % that means 8 out of 10 trades will be successful. Just as the weather forecasting can never be fully accurate; in the same way Technical Analysis can never give us truly accurate results. Researcher can just endeavour to make our success rate as high as possible by concentrating on improving the odds of making profitable trades.[9]

Although no form of analysis provides absolute certainty, numerous versions of technical analysis set up the ability to gain signal confirmation, even beyond price itself. Non-price reversals appear as volume spikes (these usually accompany big price moves) in a variety of volume signals, in moving averages and in momentum oscillators.

All reversal signals should be acted upon only if they are also accompanied with a confirmation signal. No individual signals are reliable enough to generate a trade unless the all-important confirmation signal also appears.

Beyond these basic requirements to legitimize reversal signals, the proximity issue also must be applied. In other words, a reversal signal must occur at the expected point in the price trend. A bearish reversal should be found at or close to the top of a bullish trend. As the trend is exhausted and price pauses, look for the bearish signal and confirmation. A bullish reversal should be found at the bottom of a downtrend in the same manner, pointing to the exhaustion point of the current trend. The most likely point in the price pattern to find reversals is at or close to resistance (bearish reversal) or support (bullish reversal). This observation is confirmed by one highly detailed analysis that "reversals occur most often near price extremes."[10]

Proximity of the reversal must occur at these indicated points, or they cannot be used reliably to enter a trade. Some literature about technical analysis claims that when a reversal signal appears in the wrong place, it acts as a continuation signal. A signal normally called a bearish reversal that is seen at the bottom of a downtrend would be considered bearish continuation in this interpretation, and a bullish signal at the top is treated as a bullish continuation signal.

This interpretation is questionable. It is especially popular among candlestick literature. If it is to be believed, a candlestick can be either reversal or continuation, depending on where it resides within the current price pattern. However, this is a questionable belief. A signal appearing in the wrong place, in fact, is not a signal of any kind, but a coincidence of pattern formation. The multiple-session signal formed under candlestick analysis is not entirely reliable by itself. Formations often occur as coincidence in price patterns. The only reliable rules of interpretation include:

1. A reversal must appear at the right point in the trading range.
2. The reversal must be confirmed before acting on what it indicates.
3. Reversal is most likely at or close to resistance or support.

Proximity in Consolidation Trends

The previously discussed "flip" between resistance and support is witnessed often on charts. When a previous support level becomes new resistance (or vice versa), it adds considerable strength to a new trading range.

This flip occurs often after an extended consolidation trend. This trend consists of range-bound prices and eventually ends with a successful breakout. The breakout is also likely to follow a failed move in the opposite direction. For example, a breakout above resistance fails, but leads to a successful breakout below support. Figure 2.3 presents a consolidation trend of four months, with trading between resistance of $46 and support of $44.65.

A breakout above resistance took place in mid-November but immediately failed. This failure was signaled by a candlestick reversal signal known as a three inside down. This was confirmed by a retreat into the established trading range, as well as by a price gap and a long black day. In this example, the proximity of price to the established consolidation trend was the significant attribute of the failed breakout. The immediate appearance of the bearish reversal made failure likely; confirmation added to the likely failure.

What happened next further revealed the nature of breakout from consolidation and what is required for the breakout to succeed. Figure 2.4 contains an expansion of the same chart for an additional two months.

Fig. 2.3 Consolidation trend

Fig. 2.4 Consolidation trend with breakout

An exceptionally strong move took place above resistance, consisting of eight consecutive white candlesticks. This is an unusual pattern known as *eight new price lines*. Consecutive white sessions create a bearish reversal signal. The bearish move back into range followed with another long black candle, confirming the bearish move.

This signal is complex and can be interpreted in many ways. Like so many candlestick signals, its value depends on where it appears within a trend, and what preceded it. In the example, the eight new price lines set up a breakout.

The likely bearish reversal was made especially strong for two reasons. First, breakout itself is likely to lead to retracement back into the previous range. Second, it moved price substantially higher than previous resistance. Even so, the signal itself—without knowing what happens next—is both unusual and controversial:

> The formation of eight new highs in the price ... has an implication that the market will be getting tired, and it may be a good time to take profits before a reversal. In some ways, you may think that this is against the old trading adage of "cutting your losses, and letting your profits run," and whether it is good advice depends on the particular circumstances.[11]

However, this was not merely a failed bullish breakout. It set up a successful bearish breakout initially signaled by the strong price move below previous support. The new trading range was established by a flip from previous support to new resistance. This was tested by mid-February when a session gapped strongly above resistance but immediately declined to close below. The result: a new consolidation trend below the previous one.

Risks in Every Strategy

The purpose in examining the various attributes of proximity has been to establish the importance of charting in the selection of a long-term LEAPS option, as well as in the timing of entry and exit in the series of short-term options opened to reduce the LEAPS basis to zero. This strategy contains risks and, like all strategies, those risks must be understood in context of whether your risk tolerance is a good match for the strategy:

> The enormous popularity of option contracts has arisen, in part, because options allow investors to precisely tailor their risks to their preferences ... Understanding option returns is important because options have remarkable risk-return characteristics.[12]

This point is not lost on options traders familiar with a complex range of risks. Consider the risks of the installment purchase. This consists of a long call with many months before expiration, and a series of short-term short positions, either calls or puts. The selection of short options should depend on proximity of price to the edges of the trading range. The risk to the long LEAPS call is that price will decline below the strike, and the associated risk that the short positions will not cover the initial cost. If you open a LEAPS put, the risk is that price will eventually end up above the strike and the short positions will not cover the cost.

A more serious risk involves possible exercise of short puts or calls. If a short put is exercised, you are required to buy 100 shares at the strike, which would be higher than the current price. You end up with inflated stock, meaning you need to sell at a loss or hold in the hopes of a price reversal. Exercise risk is avoided by setting up a buffer between price and strike and monitoring the position and being prepared to roll forward if it goes in the money.

If you open a short call, the same rules apply. However, because this is a diagonal spread, the short calls are "covered" in a sense by the longer term LEAPS position, if a call. If the LEAPS is a put, the short call is uncovered. In either case, exercise could result in a disparity between the strikes of the long and short positions. Using the LEAPS call to satisfy exercise of a short call would be likely to leave a net debit.

All these risks exist in every strategy. In the case of an installment calendar spread, risk is avoided through constant monitoring and diligence, and determining how to act to counter exercise risk. In the case of using short calls for either strategy, avoid the week of ex-dividend date. This is the most likely period for early exercise. In the case of using either calls or puts, also avoid being exposed on the short side during the week of an earnings announcement, and surprises could move the short position in the money, presenting a considerable challenge.

The idea of the short positions is to roll them from week to week, taking small profits while reducing exposure to risk. However, you also need to be aware of the risks faced any time short options are open, especially when markets are volatile. This does not mean the installment strategies should be avoided. It does mean you have to remain diligent and track positions to look for a time to close. The ideal outcome is to close at a profit; other alternatives are to close at breakeven or even at a net loss, or to roll forward when the short option has moved in the money.

Collateral Requirements

The offset between a long LEAPS position and a short-term short position is not unlimited. Some traders may rationalize that a strategy presenting a good idea with single contracts can be just as effectively put into place with 10 or 100 contracts. However, collateral requirements will restrict your ability to expand the strategy.

Under collateral rules, you are required to post an initial margin and maintain it based on subsequent price movement. A covered position (like a covered call) requires no options margin; an uncovered option requires posting of cash or securities. If your margin falls below the required level, your brokerage firm will dispose of some of your open positions to satisfy the requirement.

Valuable Resources: The Chicago Board Options Exchange (CBOE) publishes a free *Margin Manual* that explains requirements for every strategy. You can download this publication at http://www.cboe.com/LearnCenter/pdf/margin2-00.pdf

The CBOE also publishes a free margin calculator, enabling you to plug in the numbers and see exactly how much you need in your margin account for a short position. This free calculator can be downloaded at http://www.cboe.com/trading-tools/calculators/margin-calculator

Options and Market Risk

The installment strategies work to effectively hedge market risk. If you want to freeze today's price for future purchase of stock, the installment call or *contingent purchase* plan is worth examining. You later can exercise the ITM LEAPS call with its zero basis and buy shares of stock below market value.

The *risk hedge* is set up when you buy a LEAPS put. This is most appropriate if you own 100 shares of stock and want to eliminate future market risk. Assuming the offsetting short positions will take the basis in the put down to zero, this installment strategy eliminates all market risk below the put's strike. For example, if you open a 24-month LEAPS put with the idea of protecting your initial investment, the installment accomplishes that goal. If the market value of shares falls below your basis, a strike at the same level allows you to sell shares at (or above) your basis and avoid a net loss. Beyond using your original basis to pick a strike, if share value has risen above your basis, the risk hedge makes even more sense. You can protect your basis *and* appreciated value with the installment put.

The purpose in the installment strategy is to avoid losses in future price movement by freezing price of shares (for future purchase) or eliminating market risk (with the risk hedge). In creating and maintaining your portfolio, risk management is the best use of options. In the past, options were considered as strictly speculative vehicles. Increasingly, traders and investors now use options to hedge risk or to freeze future purchase prices.

Even with the significant advantages in hedging the price of the underlying, the market risks of both long and short positions should not be overlooked. Risk is unavoidable, but in the case of the installment strategy, they can be avoided. By picking high-quality companies, you reduce exposure to both fundamental and technical volatility. By setting up proximity of options entry and exit to exploit the trading range, you improve profitable outcomes. By also creating a buzzer between current price and strike, you reduce chances for exercise, notably when exercise comes up in one to two weeks.

It begins with the selection of the highest quality companies. The idea of *value investing* has been overused and it is not defined in the same way by every investor. For the installment strategy, identifying a limited list of fundamental trends and indicators is an essential first step. Whether you already own shares or want to purchase shares in the future, starting with selection of a company and its stock is where the installment strategy begins.

Notes

1. Natenberg, S. (1994). *Option Volatility & Pricing*. New York: McGraw-Hill, p. 95.
2. Chung, K.; Seongkyu, G.; & Doojin, R. (July 2016). Trade duration, informed trading, and option moneyness. *International Review of Economics & Finance*, Volume 44, pp. 395–411.
3. Roll, R.; Schwartz, E.; & Avanidhar S. (April 2010). O/S: The relative trading activity in options and stock. *Journal of Financial Economics*, Volume 96, Issue 1, pp. 1–17.
4. An, Y. & Suo, W. (Winter 2009). An empirical comparison of option-pricing models in hedging exotic options. *Financial Management*, Vol. 38, No. 4, pp. 889–914.
5. Snyder, G. (Jan.-Feb., 1967). A look at options. *Financial Analysts Journal*. Volume 23, No. 1, pp. 100–103.
6. Nison, S. (2001). *Japanese Candlestick Charting Techniques*, 2nd ed. New York: New York Institute of Finance, pp. 6–7.
7. Tabell, E. & Tabell, A. (March–April 1964). The Case for Technical Analysis. *Financial Analysts Journal*, Volume 20, No. 2, pp. 67–76.
8. Hoffland, D. (May–June, 1967). The Folklore of Wall Street. *Financial Analysts Journal*, Volume 23, No. 3, pp. 85–88.
9. Garg, B. (October 2014). Technical analysis indicators: Pathway towards rewarding journey. *International Journal of Management and Social Sciences Research*, Volume 3, No. 10, pp. 87–93.
10. Bulkowski, T. (2008). *Encyclopedia of Candlestick Charts*. Hoboken NJ: John Wiley & Sons, p. 12.
11. Northcott, A. (2009). *The Complete Guide to Using Candlestick Charting*. Ocala FL: Atlantic Publishing Group, p. 237.
12. Coval, J., & Shumway, T. (June 2001). Expected option returns. *The Journal of Finance*, Volume 56, No. 3, pp. 983–1009.

3

Picking the Right Stock

The installment strategy is intended to accomplish one of two objectives. For those currently holding equity positions, the LEAPS put eliminates all market risk, and the put is paid for with a series of very short-term short options, either calls or puts. For those interested in future price appreciation (either to buy shares or to benefit from price appreciation of the option), the LEAPS call freezes the future underlying price at the LEAPS strike. This means that even with substantial price appreciation, shares of the underlying can be purchased at the strike.

In both cases, the quality of the underlying fundamentals defines value investments. Applying an installment option strategy should be limited to only the strongest companies in terms of capitalization, cash flow and profits. Otherwise, why invest in shares and why devise a system for future purchase? The distinction between fundamentally strong and weak companies leads to the decision about which options to open. It is the same qualifying process for buying stock even without the inclusion of options for risk hedging.

Investors who prefer buying shares of smaller, fundamentally volatile companies are speculators, although they often deny this label. These fundamentally weak companies are likely to perform exceptionally well or exceptionally poorly, depending on the direction of movement in the broader market:

> Portfolios invested in small, growing, highly levered companies, for example, are often so sensitive to market movements that a 10 per cent rise (or fall) in the general market level will cause a 20 per cent rise (or fall) in the value of the portfolio. When one manages this kind of portfolio it is very easy to convince oneself (and others) that one is a trading genius when the market is going up.[1]

Fundamental volatility affects technical risk directly, and therefore the starting point for an installment strategy should be selection of fundamentally exceptionally strong companies.

Fundamental Risk

A lot of emphasis is put on *technical* risk, the price-related market risks for any listed company's stock. If shares are purchased and the price subsequently declines, you have a paper loss. In that case, you must wait for price to rebound, or you must devise a risk hedge to offset that loss.

Technical risk, for many traders, is the sole focus for options trading. A volatile stock offers higher option premiums, so short-term sales of options brings in more premium dollars, but also comes with accelerated market risk. A low-volatility stock has lower option premiums and is associated with lower risks.

This would imply that high volatility is likely to yield *better* returns for investors, but when the issues of both stock and option market risks are considered together, the opposite is true. Considering the fundamental volatility of a company as a first step and technical volatility as a second, but related step, a trade-off occurs among many options traders: higher stock risk is traded for higher option returns. A recent study points out the importance of evaluating volatility levels as a factor in stock selection. The study concluded that

> low volatility stocks earn higher returns than high volatility stocks ... volatility stocks have higher operating returns and this might explain why low volatility stocks earn higher stock returns. These results provide a partial explanation for the 'low volatility effect' that is independent from the existence of market anomalies or per se inefficiencies that might otherwise drive a low volatility effect. We emphasize the importance of controlling for stock return volatility when analyzing operating performance and stock performance.[2]

This observation defies common beliefs, especially among options traders, that high volatility is a positive attribute, especially for short options. However, if that same high volatility defines higher risk, lower return stocks, is high volatility as attractive? The answer depends on the timing of trade entry and exit. Because volatility is not fixed but tends to increase or decrease cyclically, timing of all trades—both long and short—may be based on a combination of technical signals and the volatility trend.

In addition to the technical side, fundamental risk should not be ignored. Most traders will agree that trading options without a comparison of risks (on the technical side) would not make sense; this observation includes historical and implied volatility. However, the fundamental risk is equally important. This refers to several attributes, including:

1. **Volatility in basic annual trends involving fundamental results.** The concept of "fundamental volatility" refers to the trend itself. Is revenue increasing one year and decreasing the next? Is the price/earnings (P/E) ratio remaining within a predictable high-to-low annual range? Are dividends per shares changing each year, or are they flat or declining? Is the level of long-term debt increasing, decreasing or flat? Fundamental volatility makes it difficult, if not impossible, to determine whether the organization is being well managed.
2. **Questions of whether fundamental indicators are improving, flat or declining.** The current level of reported fundamental measurements may be improving, flat or declining. This is the most effective test of fundamental volatility. In the best of circumstances, you want to see revenue and earnings growing each year and the degree of net return (earnings divided by revenues) reported consistently within a narrow range.
3. **Reliability of fundamental trends, including signals of weakening or exposed profitability, cash flow or capitalization issues.** Once a trend is established, seeing it continue year after year is reassuring. Just as technical trends give you a sense of reliability, fundamental trends are just as revealing. There are only four areas where fundamental trends need to be tracked to identify high-quality companies. These are (a) dividend yield and trends, (b) P/E annual ranges, (c) revenue and earnings trends and (d) debt to total capitalization ratio.
4. **Overall strength or weakness of the company, measured by fundamental aspects currently and over past years.** The final attribute, beyond analyzing the trend itself, is the identification of fundamentally strong or weak organizations. A "strong" organization increases dividend per share every year, while holding long-term debt to the same percentage of total capitalization, or even declining. It also reports higher revenues each year and consistent earnings, both in terms of dollars and net return. It also reports annual P/E ratio range from high to low at moderate levels.

The Effect of Fundamental Trends on Options Risk

In the unending effort to quantify options trading, how do options traders determine what is a high or a low risk? In fact, many influences affect fundamental trends and, as a result, the level of options risk. Options traders who pay attention to fundamentals may easily overlook the complexity of this, and it is natural to assume that there is only one fundamental volatility defined over the underlying asset and all its derivatives. This is because information which affects the fundamentals of the underlying asset is the same across all derivatives of the asset and, thus, results in the same fundamental volatility. Other factors will also influence this single fundamental volatility as well as information arrival: the structure of related markets, the distribution of assets held by investors, transaction costs and numerous other factors in the global economy, including all the macroeconomic information available at the time.[3]

Defining high or low risk must consider an understanding that fundamental analysis cannot be limited to a test of ratios and trends in financial reports; more subtle influences directly impact option risk. Complicating this evaluation, the effort to identify risk usually is specific to a strategy. For example, a covered call is classified as "low risk" and an uncovered call is classified as "high risk." This is an imperfect method, however. In some cases, the classification is not accurate. For example, if an underlying price has declined to the bottom of the trading range, timing for a covered call is poor. The true risks of opening a covered call at this point include:

1. Opening a position below your original basis, so that exercise would create a net capital loss.
2. A reversal and move above the strike represents a lost opportunity risk, because exercise occurs at the strike; so higher current value is sacrificed.
3. A move in the money could result in rolling forward. This ties up capital for a longer period and prevents you from pursuing other trades.
4. Limited potential: the covered call's best outcome is for profit equal to the net credit received for opening the covered call. Waiting for price to develop often translates to stronger profits in the underlying.

The same argument can be applied to uncovered calls. When a stock's price gaps far above the current trading range (e.g. due to an unusually strong positive earnings surprise), it is likely that the price will reverse to fill the gap. At this point in the price behavior, an uncovered call is not as risky as it would be at mid-range or at the bottom of the range.

The point is that "risk" is not fixed by the characteristics of a strategy. Even when the strategy includes potential for unlimited loss (e.g. with an uncovered call), the true risk relies on historical volatility (a factor influenced by the fundamentals) and proximity of price to the borders of the trading range.

To quantify options risk, observing historical volatility is a worthwhile starting point. This does not mean that every trader should ignore the inherent risks associated with a strategy. However, an understanding of risk begins with analysis of fundamental volatility. Two observations can be made concerning how fundamentals affect option risks. First, companies with strong fundamental trends (low volatility) tend to also experience low technical trends (low price volatility), and to perform better than market averages. Second, because companies with strong fundamentals are well managed, the options traded on those companies tend to be reliable in the market, meaning lower than average bid/ask spreads and a more robust market participation in trading options.

The tendency for well-managed companies with strong fundamentals to translate to strong technical signals further defines options risk. Combining these factors with technical analysis of the current trend leads to improved selection and timing of options trends.

On the other end of the risk spectrum, companies with high volatility in their fundamental trends represent greater risk, both for the stock and its options. High volatility is seen in revenue and earnings trending in unpredictable ways, in low or skipped dividends, in exceptionally high P/E ranges, or large changes from year to year, and in high or increasing levels of long-term debt that outpace growth in profits. These fundamentally volatile companies will experience correspondingly high historical volatility as well.

This comparison is significant for options traders. Because high-risk (volatile) stocks tend to have richer options premiums, these often are the options of choice. Why? Because higher volatility and higher premium are viewed by many traders as better trading opportunities. The high historical and implied volatility in these options are not only attractive at first glance but also will create vulnerability due to rapid changes in value resulting from sudden price reversals.

Consequently, options traders who do not pay attention to fundamentals volatility place themselves at risk of losses. A skilled trader who relies on thorough analysis of the underlying security will also study fundamental volatility, knowing that this affects options risks directly.

Contingent Purchase and Stock Selection

Selection of one company over another, based on fundamental volatility, should be the starting point for all options trading. This is especially true when considering the contingent purchase strategy.

Because this is a time spread (also called calendar spread or horizontal spread), two attributes are in play at the same time, the long-term long call and a series of short-term short calls or puts. However, the strategy goes a step beyond the typical time spread, in which the value of the spread cannot be determined until both options expire. The spread's value depends not only on where the underlying market is when the short-term option expires, but also on what will happen between that time and the time when the long-term option expires.[4]

This is an accurate description of the time spread as often entered, but only for speculating on future price movement of the underlying. Under this strategy, a short-term short option loses time value rapidly and expires or can be closed at a profit, and the longer term long option increases in value as the underlying gains value.

However, the contingent purchase strategy exploits the well-known attributes of the time spread. It is used to freeze the price of stock at a specified strike for future purchase, *and* to reduce the basis in that long-term call to zero with a series of short-term short options. Because the plan is to eventually purchase stock (or close the long call at a profit), the selection of the underlying stock is of utmost importance.

The rationale behind contingent purchase demonstrates why stock selection is the key. One of two goals are in effect with this strategy. First, you intend to buy 100 shares for each call opened, before expiration of the long call. This will occur only if the price at that time is higher than the strike, meaning you will be able to purchase shares below market value. Second, you might decide to sell the call at a profit as an alternative to buying shares.

Neither of these outcomes will be realized if the price per share is lower than the LEAPS strike. However, in this outcome, you do not suffer a loss because the call's premium was offset by profits from selling options between inception and expiration.

The rationale, therefore, is based on the belief that the stock will be more valuable in the future than it is today. This implies that you also believe the company is fundamentally strong and will report consistent trends, leading to strong growth in the stock price. A contingent purchase could be initiated on any company on which options are available, but the point is to select companies with exceptional growth prospects.

A second rationale for entering the positing is to hedge against the possibility of price decline. Any stock can rise or fall, so even what appears to be a strong candidate today could be a disappointment in the future. If you can freeze today's price for the coming year with a LEAPS call, and pay for that call before it expires, you overcome the market risk completely. That risk is that the stock price could fall. If you simply buy shares today and the price declines, you have a paper loss. You can sell and realize the loss or wait in the hope that price will rebound. Unfortunately, many investors end up with a portfolio of depreciated stocks by suffering losses and not realizing a recovery. The contingent purchase solves this problem. If the stock price declines, the LEAPS call can be sold or allowed to expire without losing any money.

This rationale supports the contention that fundamental volatility matters. For many investors, selection of a company and purchase of its stock often is not based on any detailed analysis, either fundamental or technical. A few years ago, before General Motors (GM) filed for bankruptcy, many investors bought stock because GM was considered the gem of the auto industry. "I like General Motors and I own one of their cars" was an example of how some investors picked GM over all other companies.

The same applies to all decisions to select one company over another. "I invest in Kodak because they are the leaders in the film industry" might have been an equally compelling justification for buying their stock. As true as the statement was, the film industry was eclipsed by the emerging digital camera market and Kodak did not realize this soon enough to avoid bankruptcy. This was ironic considering that Kodak developed the first digital camera in 1975—and then ignored its potential. Their stock fell from about $80 per share in 1998 to nearly 0 at the end of 2011.[5]

The sensible method for picking a company is based on analysis of fundamental trends and identification of exceptional *value* as a first step, and then checking technical indicators, including historical volatility to time trades. The system of selecting options trades based on name recognition of the company, personal likes or dislikes and other criteria not remotely related to quality is a poor method for deciding which underlying securities to pick—whether to invest in stock and trade conservatively, or to speculate with options.

Contingent Sales as Risk Hedges of Stock

The logic of picking companies based on fundamental strength also applies to risk hedging. This strategy is most likely to be put into action when you own shares of stock. The purpose of the installment strategy using long-term long LEAPS puts is to eliminate all market risk below the put's strike.

Just as the contingent purchase time spread (with a LEAPS call purchased) is popularly understood as a speculative strategy, the risk hedge (with a LEAPS put purchased) often is not considered. Rather, the time spread with the long put is viewed as a high-risk speculative trade, with the observation that "since LEAPS are long-term and therefore expensive, one is generally taking on a large debit in such a spread and may have substantial risk if the stock performs adversely."[6]

This is factual but based solely on the use of a put-based time spread as a speculative strategy. When the spread is opened as a risk hedge utilizing a series of short installment payments, the profile becomes more conservative, if stock selection is the starting point and that shares held in the portfolio are for high-quality companies. The question concerning whether to open a risk hedge using puts begins with analysis of stocks and the companies they represent. Why are you holding shares of the company? Are they fundamentally exceptional and worth keeping shares? Is the stock volatile? Has it risen or fallen in value since the date of purchase?

If the company in which you own shares is not exceptional in terms of fundamental trends, who keep the stock? If it has risen in value, the sensible move is to sell shares and replace them with shares of a stronger, better-managed and more profitable company. If the value of the investment has declined, consider taking the loss now and moving your investment to a stronger company's stock. As an alternative, can you buy a LEAPS put at or above your original basis? If so, you can create a risk hedge and later decide whether to exercise the put and sell shares (escaping the position without a loss) or sell the put and offset the loss in stock (if the put is in the money by expiration).

If the company is an exceptional fundamental choice, the risk hedge using puts makes perfect sense. This hedge eliminates market risk below the put's strike, so that the strike should be at or above your original purchase price. This provides you the choice of selling the put if the price declines or exercising it and selling at the strike even when the underlying price has declined.

The most logical timing of the risk hedge is when a high-quality company's stock has appreciated since your purchase. This presents a dilemma, especially if you would like to continue holding shares. For example, a high-dividend stock with rising revenues and profits, moderate P/E range and steady or declining long-term debt is worth keeping in your portfolio. However, if price has appreciated, are you at risk of losing the paper profits? In this situation, you will be tempted to sell shares and take profits even though the company continues to represent a strong investment.

The alternative is the risk hedge. Buying a long-term LEAPS put at a strike at or above your original cost per share eliminates all market risk below the strike. (This assumes that you can pay for the put by selling a series of short-term options each week up to expiration.)

The elimination of market risk has a profound positive effect on the position. By eliminating market risk, any outcome will be profitable. If share price declines below the put's strike, you can exercise the put and sell shares at the strike. If the strike is higher than your original cost per share, the difference between purchase price and put strike represents a capital gain. You can also sell the put and take profits, which will consist of intrinsic value and offset the paper loss in stock—also reducing your basis in the shares.

If the price per share has risen above the put's strike, you can sell the put at a profit (the net basis should be zero by the time this decision is made, due to your having sold short options each week). Or you can let the put expire. In either case, the time you owned the put allowed you to escape market risk entirely.

The selection of a company as a candidate for the risk hedge should include several criteria:

1. It should be a company you would like to continue owning, and on which you expect long-term price appreciation to continue.
2. The put's strike must be at or above the original cost per share. A price above the net cost is advantageous. If you exercise the put before expiration, you will sell shares at a price above your original cost.
3. The company should be fundamentally exceptional based on a short list of fundamental criteria. If it is not, the sensible decision is to sell shares and replace them with shares of a company meeting the fundamental criteria.

Dividend Yield and Trends

In the analysis of stock selection, the first fundamental trend to examine is the dividend yield. This is measured in two ways. First, the dividend yield should be higher than average. Limiting your search to companies paying 3.5 percent or more is a strong starting point. Second, limit your search to companies that have increased dividend per share in each of the past ten years or more.

Dividend yield should not be analyzed as an attribute of stock selection separate from other fundamental tests. The association between dividends and return on investment is acknowledged in the literature, and one study concluded that "returns and dividend yields over time and ... at least part of this relation can be attributed to dividend-related changes in risk measures."[7]

This relationship often is overlooked or ignored. The dividend yield often is misunderstood by traders and investors, and the importance of dividends as a portion of total return is overlooked as a minor contributor to outcomes. In truth, dividend yield at or above 3.5 percent is likely to represent a major portion of return. As a selection criterion, two companies whose fundamental strength is otherwise similar may be narrowed down based on dividend yield and trends in dividends per share.

The yield you will earn on your investment is always going to be the yield based on the price you paid per share, no matter how much time has passed, and no matter how the price per share has changed. A focus on *current* dividend yield is distracting if you already own shares, because this does not affect either your basis in shares or the yield you earn.

Table 3.1 Dividend per share comparison

Fiscal year	Dividend per share Coca-Cola ($)	PG&E ($)
2008	0.76	1.56
2009	0.82	1.68
2010	0.88	1.82
2011	0.94	1.82
2012	1.02	1.82
2013	1.12	1.82
2014	1.22	1.82
2015	1.32	1.82
2016	1.40	1.93
2017	1.48	1.55

Source: CFRA Stock Reports

The two criteria should be checked together. A yield of 3.5 percent or more, combined with increasing dividends per share in each of the last ten years, defines a strong company, if long-term debt has not been increased to fund those dividend payments.

A comparison of dividends per share over ten years, between two companies, shows how trends develop. Coca-Cola (KO) increased its dividend every year, but Pacific Gas & Electric or PG&E (PCG) paid a flat dividend for several years, with the last two years declining. This is summarized in Table 3.1.

Debt to Total Capitalization Ratio and Trend

A comparison between dividends and long-term debt is an often-invisible test of fundamental strength. Even though this comparison might not be considered by an analyst, it is the most important fundamental test and should always be performed.

The ratio is discovered by dividing long-term debt by total capitalization. It is a percentage but is normally reported numerically, in round numbers and without percentage signs. For example, if long-term debt at the end of the fiscal year is reported (in millions of dollars) as $42,618 and total capitalization (also in millions) is $109,440, the ratio is:

$$42,618 \div 109,440 = 39$$

The long-term debt in this example represents 39 percent of total capitalization, meaning that shareholders' equity represents 61 percent. "Total" capitalization is the combined long-term debt and shareholders' equity, so the test of long-term debt trends is crucial in identifying the strength or weakness of a company.

In some cases, corporations reporting annual net losses continue to increase dividends per share, which is puzzling on its surface. However, these annual increases in dividends during years of negative earnings might be financed by ever-higher long-term debt. This not only damages equity share of total capitalization over the long term but is contrary to the belief in the relationship between dividends and shareholder interests. One paper stated that

> one of the most important reasons for investors and companies to focus on dividends is the relationship between dividends and equity value: The value of equities should reflect the discounted future value of dividends.[8]

This relationship often is ignored or discounted by corporations and in extreme cases, long-term debt could grow so that equity value declined *below zero*, and more than 100 percent of total capitalization was represented by long-term debt.

Returning to the previous puzzle about increasing dividends: if the company continues to increase its dividend per share year after year but at the same time reports net losses, how can it afford to increase the dividend? This question, rarely asked by analysts, should always be asked because in the extreme case, producing the positive appearance of growing dividends at the cost of replacing equity with long-term debt damages equity interests. Higher debt means that future earnings will have to go toward debt service at a higher rate than in the past, and ultimately, shareholders will see diminishing earnings due to ever-higher interests on the debt. Future dividends will decline and use of earnings as working capital or to fund expansion will be minimized.

When long-term debt grows over time, it is a danger signal, especially if debt is accumulated to pay for dividends when earnings are inadequate for that purpose. Even if a company is profitable, when dividends are too high to pay from earnings, allowing long-term debt to rise is a troubling trend.

An example: Sears Holding (SHLD) declined in capital strength and profitability for several years. As of April 12, 2018, the chart of SHLD revealed a dismal picture for investors. This is summarized in Fig. 3.1.

The chart reveals a declining trendline since August 1, eight months earlier. Over this period, Sears lost 66 percent of its share value. Why? An analysis of the long-term debt trend shows that SHLD has *negative* equity, due to ever-higher long-term debt. A five-year summary of the debt trend is shown in Table 3.2.

With $354 million negative equity, Sears was relying completely on long-term debt. This explains the decline in value of stock over time. SHLD, valued above $82 per share in April 2008, lost most of its share value along with the disappearance of its equity.[9]

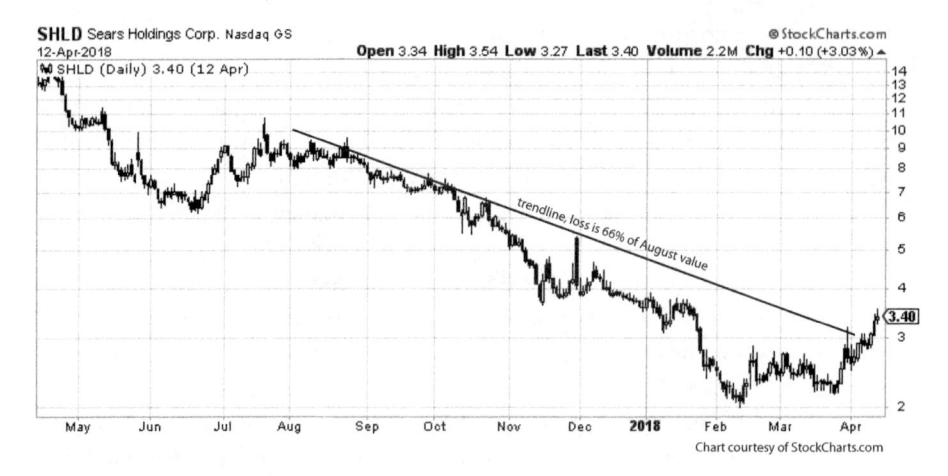

Fig. 3.1 Sears Holding stock chart, one year

Table 3.2 Sears long-term debt trend

	In millions of dollars		
Fiscal year	Long-term debt ($)	Total capitalization ($)	Ratio
2013	1943	4698	41
2014	2559	4298	60
2015	2877	1926	149
2016	1971	8	246
2017	3470	−354	980

Source: CFRA Stock Reports

This was an extreme example, but it has occurred often in the market. Once known as the most influential of the Blue Chip stocks, Sears, along with GM, Eastman Kodak and many others, lost its equity value. The warning sign—increasing net losses and growing dependence on long-term debt—shows that when this begins, the value of a company as a potential investment declines.

As a fundamental ratio and trend, growing long-term debt should eliminate a company from consideration as a candidate for either form of the installment strategy. When you consider the short list of high-value companies that can produce profits to increase dividends per share *and* hold long-term debt level or declining, there is no need to invest in companies whose level of long-term debt is on the rise.

The comparison of the debt to equity ratio and dividend yield is revealing. For example, McDonalds (MCD) increased its dividend over ten years by a substantial margin of 135 percent, from $1.63 per share in 2008 up to

Table 3.3 Comparison, debt and dividend trends

	McDonalds (MCD)		Walmart (WMT)	
Fiscal year	Debt	Dividend ($)	Debt	Dividend ($)
2008	43	1.63	29	0.95
2009	43	2.05	29	1.09
2010	44	2.26	34	1.21
2011	45	2.53	34	1.46
2012	47	2.87	28	1.59
2013	47	3.12	30	1.88
2014	54	3.28	30	1.92
2015	77	3.44	29	1.96
2016	109	3.61	29	2.00
2017	112	3.83	24	2.04

Source: CFRA Stock Reports

$3.83 in 2017. However, its long-term debt rose in the same period from 43 to 112, growth of 160 percent. That is a negative trend, with debt over 100 percent of total capital in the last two years. In comparison, Walmart (WMT) increased its dividend every year from 0.95 in 2008 up to 2.04 in 2017, an increase of 115 percent. At the same time, long-term debt to total capitalization did not change very much from year to year, and from 2008 to 2017, fell from 29 down to 24.

The comparison of the debt to equity ratio and annual dividends is summarized in Table 3.3.

If only dividend per share was subject to review, MCD was a preferable choice. Dividend per share was substantially higher each year than WMT's payment. And the dividend yield for MCD as of 2017 was 2.50 percent (on April 13, 2018) versus WMT's yield of 2.42 percent. With MCD's dividend slightly better but dividend per share substantially higher, a review of only the dividend side of the picture tells only part of the story.

When the debt to total capitalization is added in, the picture changes. MCD reported debt above 100 percent of total equity, whereas WMT held long-term debt down to less than one-fourth of total capitalization.

In picking companies as candidates for installment strategies, this comparison shows that the complete fundamental review must include both dividend and debt trends. In the interest of long-term capitalization, it would have been prudent for MCD to reduce or even skip its dividend and bring debt under control. However, under prevailing accounting rules, there is no restriction on increasing long-term debt to fund ever-higher dividends. But in selecting companies for high quality on a fundamental basis, MCD would have to be rejected based on its climbing long-term debt.

P/E Annual Ranges

The P/E ratio is an unusual indicator, as it combines a technical signal (price) with a fundamental signal (earnings).

P/E is widely misunderstood. A tendency to review a current P/E only ignores the impact of annual ranges from low to high P/E, and even more critical, the longer term annual range of the P/E ratio. Part of the blame for this is the emphasis on price per share rather than on the true return to investors:

> Users of financial statements ... really want an earnings figure that measures value, not change in value. Analysts, for example, want an earnings number they can multiply by a standard price-earnings ratio to arrive at an estimate of the firm's value. Accordingly, the ideal set of accounting rules is one that makes the price-earnings ratio as constant as possible.[10]

As much as analysts (and investors) might desire consistency in the P/E ratio and other fundamentals, the reality is that a stock's price varies, often unpredictably and often without regard to the fundamental volatility that *should* influence price volatility. This makes a single P/E multiple unreliable because it measures a moment in time, and uses two dissimilar factors (current price per share versus last quarter's or last year's earnings per share).

With these variables in mind, the more reliable method for utilizing P/E is to analyze annual ranges from high to low, and spot trends as well as volatility levels. A company reporting consistent mid-range P/E is a more likely candidate for strategies such as installment purchase or sale, and highly volatile ranges of P/E represent greater fundamental *and* technical volatility.

A comparison between two companies—Lockheed Martin (LMT) and Microsoft (MSFT)—shows how low-to-high P/E can vary over a ten-year period, as shown in Table 3.4.

Table 3.4 P/E ratio trend comparison

Fiscal year	LMT Low	LMT High	MSFT Low	MSFT High
2008	9	16	15	24
2009	7	11	8	16
2010	9	12	12	20
2011	9	12	9	13
2012	10	12	9	12
2013	10	16	10	18
2014	16	20	12	19
2015	17	20	16	20
2016	18	23	18	43
2017	19	26	25	42

Source: CFRA Stock Reports

In the case of LMT, the range from low to high gradually increased, but remained in the moderate range between 10 and 25. Since this multiple represents the number of years of current earnings reflected in price, investors prefer this moderate range over the long term.

In comparison, MSFT's low-to-high P/E was more volatile. In the last two reported years, the range increased substantially. In 2017, the high of 42 means the stock is overpriced. Based on the latest reported earnings per share (EPS) at the time, the current price was equal to 42 years of earnings.

Revenue and Earnings Trends

Although technicians spend a great deal of time focused on revenue and earnings trends, these are only part of the bigger story. Including dividend per share, debt to total capitalization and annual range of the P/E ratio complete the analysis.

Earnings as reported are not consistent between organizations. Accounting rules are easily interpreted in a different manner from one company to another, and the variation can be significant. The use of earnings numbers cannot be isolated to a single fiscal period but must be studied as part of a long-term trend. This is the only way to smooth out year-to-year accounting decisions. Reported earnings

> Are often the product of deliberate choices between various accounting treatments and business options ... The quality of a reported earnings figure can be lowered if management recognizes revenues or expenditures either prematurely or belatedly, or chooses a liberal accounting treatment over a more conservative one.[11]

A familiarity with accounting rules under the Generally Accepted Accounting Principles (GAAP) system realizes that "earnings" can be subjected to a broad range of interpretations, within the rules. Consequently, the most recent fiscal year's results cannot be taken in isolation as typical of performance. A ten-year comparison of earnings is needed to spot trends that will smooth out year-to-year accounting decisions. The ten-year comparative study should observe three trends. The first two are revenue and earnings dollar amount. The third is the net return, or earnings as a percentage of revenue. If both revenue and earnings rise each year, it is a positive sign. But if net return is flat or declining, it could reveal weakening quality in the organization. If costs and expenses outpace growth in revenue, the long-term value of the company could potentially decline.

The inclusion of net return is essential to decide whether a company is maintaining its margins or allowing those margins to slip, or whether these results are exceptionally volatile. Few organizations will be able to report dollar growth in revenue and earnings every year without exception, which further makes the point that including net return in the analysis adds to an overall definition of value. Consistency is essential in calculating net return. The "net earnings" reported should be after-tax "net" rather than net operating (pre-tax) income.

A comparison between Wells Fargo (WFC) and Citigroup (C) reveals considerable differences over a ten-year period. This is summarized in Table 3.5.

Wells Fargo reported consistent net return and, for nine of the ten years, a narrow range of revenue. In comparison, Citigroup's results were volatile, with three years reporting net losses, and net return ranging widely.

This comparison shows that the dollar value of revenue and earnings is not complete until the net return is also calculated. Wells Fargo saw gradually increasing net return for the period, but Citigroup failed to establish a reliable trend, either in dollar amounts or in net return.

The overall fundamental analysis of a company cannot be limited to any one or two standards, nor to only one or two fiscal years. The level of an indicator is meaningful only when reviewed as an entry within a longer term trend. The combination of trends in dividends, long-term debt, P/E ratio ranges and the revenue and earnings trend collectively define whether a company represents a "value" investment for the installment strategies.

Table 3.5 Revenue and earnings comparisons

	Wells Fargo (WFC)			Citigroup (C)		
Fiscal year	Revenue (millions $)	Earnings (millions $)	Return (%)	Revenue (millions $)	Earnings (millions $)	Return (%)
2008	41,880	2655	6.3	56,499	−22,684	−49.0
2009	89,676	12,275	13.7	80,285	−1606	−2.0
2010	85,095	12,362	14.5	86,602	10,602	12.2
2011	80,965	15,869	19.6	77,331	11,067	14.3
2012	86,056	18,897	22.0	69,190	7541	10.9
2013	83,765	21,878	26.1	76,724	13,659	17.8
2014	84,375	23,057	27.3	77,219	7310	9.5
2015	86,132	22,894	26.6	76,354	17,242	22.6
2016	88,311	21,938	24.8	69,875	14,912	21.3
2017	88,517	22,183	25.1	71,780	−6798	−9.5

Source: CFRA Stock Reports

Notes

1. Bagehot, W. (March–April 1971). The only game in town. *Financial Analysts Journal*, pp. 12–22.
2. Dutt, T. & Humphery-Jenner, M. (March 2013). Stock return volatility, operating performance and stock returns: International evidence on drivers of the 'low volatility' anomaly. *Journal of Banking & Finance*, Volume 37, Issue 3, pp. 999–1017.
3. Hwang, S. & Satchell, S. (May 2000). Market risk and the concept of fundamental volatility: Measuring volatility across asset and derivative markets and testing for the impact of derivatives markets on financial markets. *Journal of Banking & Finance*, Volume 24, Issue 5, pp. 759–785.
4. Natenberg, S. (1994). *Option Volatility & Pricing*. New York: McGraw-Hill, p. 148.
5. http://www.relatably.com/q/kodak-stock-quotes, retrieved April 12, 2018.
6. McMillan, L. (2002). *Options as a Strategic Investment*, 4th ed. New York: New York Institute of Finance, p. 403.
7. Chen, N.; Grundy, B.; & Stambaugh, R. (January 1990). Changing risk, changing risk premiums, and dividend yield effects. *The Journal of Business*, Volume 63, No. 1, pp. S51–S70.
8. Manley, R., & Mueller-Glissmann, C. (2008). The market for dividends and related investment strategies. *Financial Analysts Journal*, Volume 64, No. 3, pp. 17–29.
9. https://www.nasdaq.com/symbol/shld/historical, retrieved April 12, 2018.
10. Black, F. (1980). The magic in earnings: Economic earnings versus accounting earnings. *Financial Analysts Journal*, Volume 36, No. 4, pp. 19–24.
11. Bernstein, L., & Siegel. J. (1979). The concept of earnings quality. *Financial Analysts Journal*, Volume 35, No. 4, pp. 72–75.

4

Timing with Well-Selected Technical Signals

The installment strategies rely not only on fundamental strength and timing but also on recognition of several technical signals. There are many. For this reason, focus should be on a short list of exceptionally strong price indicators. These include observation of the trading range bordered by resistance and support, Bollinger Bands, t-line, gaps and patterns identifying tops and bottoms. Candlesticks add further to the strength of price reversal and continuation.

Technical analysis itself is not universally understood or appreciated. There is far more than just the well-known price signal about coming reversals:

> The term "technical" in its application to the stock market means something quite different than ordinary dictionary definition. It refers to the study of the market itself as opposed to the external factors reflected in the market. Technical analysis is, in essence, the recording of the actual history of trading (including both price movement and the volume of transactions) for one stock or a group of equities, and deducing the future trend from this historical analysis.[1]

This overview of the meaning of technical analysis adds a useful perspective. It is more than just the observation of signals and interpretation of their meaning. It includes recognition of trends and, equally important, when trends are coming to an end. For context, this chapter focuses on specific signals as a starting point in a more advanced pursuit of analysis and timing of trades.

Beyond price, technical analysis also relies on volume signals, momentum oscillators and moving averages (MAs). These enrich the process of anticipating price behavior and in identifying trends. As a trend develops, one key technical skill is identifying the continuation of a current direction as well as signals that the trend is coming to an exhaustion point and is likely to reverse.

Volume is especially powerful when used as an initial signal and confirmed by price, or when used to confirm signals in price, adding a secondary signal. The role of volume trends, notably spikes, is among the strongest of signals. In this role,

> volume, information precision, and price movements relate, and ... sequences of volume and prices can be informative ... traders who use information contained in market statistics do better than traders who do not.[2]

Unfortunately, many technicians focus exclusively on price indicators and perhaps include momentum oscillators or MA signals but ignore volume and the strength of forecasting it provides. Volume improves trade timing, often as much as price signals. As a result, volume should not be ignored.

Entry and Exit Timing

Technical analysis is designed to accomplish a short list of advantages for the trader. These include recognition of strengthening or weakening trends, reversal or continuation signals and confirmation signals and improved timing of entry and exit from positions.

Entry and exit often are elusive, especially during a trend. If the trend continues, spotting reversal signals is likely to be difficult. Some false signals will appear, but unless these are confirmed by other price, volume or momentum signals, it is difficult to know whether to act on what is observed. Some retracement looks like reversal, with one difference: retracement usually involves a signal without confirmation, whereas a true reversal should be accompanied by confirmation in a second signal.

Improved entry and exit is essential for executing the second party of an installment strategy, the opening and closing of short-term short options. These are opened to pay for the LEAPS long position and may consist of calls or puts (or in more advanced versions of the strategy, combinations of both).

Guidelines for recognizing entry and exit timing:

1. *Not all signals are reliable.* Any signal appearing without confirmation is not enough to execute a trade. The requirement for confirmation exists for a reason. Solitary reversal signals are unreliable. Any traders who act with only one recognized signal (or without any signals) are likely to time their trades poorly.
2. *Trends do not always reverse immediately.* Trends do not always turn suddenly or without forecasting ahead of time. It is more likely that after a run in either direction, the trend will plateau and move sideways before turning to the other direction. This should be thought of as a signal in its own right, and if confirmed by other reversal signals, it is time to act.
3. *Unconfirmed signals are likely to be retracements than reversals.* The appearance of a reversal signal, by itself and lacking confirmation, normally signals short-term retracement, but this applies only after a swing trend has been in effect.
4. *Some signals are of questionable value, weakening what has appeared.* Be especially suspicious of some signals known to provide uncertain forecasts; even weak signals add to the overall prediction if confirmed, but by themselves, they are not strong enough to act. These include all triangles and wedges, flags and pennants (usually appearing as retracement), some candlesticks (e.g. doji formations and harami signals) and common gaps.
5. *Confirmation bias can mislead you.* When a trader begins an analysis in the belief that reversal is likely to occur in the short term, it is more likely that a signal will be found. But is that signal reliable? If not confirmed, it is not reliable, and should not serve as the basis to enter or exit a trade. Any chart reader can find a signal if confirmation bias rules the analysis and being aware of this improves chances for drawing a more scientific (and less subjective) conclusion.
6. *Signals have specific meanings, and these do not change.* Some analysts will claim that a signal can be either a reversal or a continuation. This is especially the case in candlestick analysis. However, signals identified as reversals do not provide confirmation when they appear in the wrong place in the trend. Some patterns appear as coincidence or mere chance, and do not always constitute a true signal.
7. *Proximity is the key to finding strong signals.* As price approaches resistance or support, the signals identified are more reliable than those appearing at mid-range. A reversal signal can appear at any point within the current trading range, but the point about proximity is that as price moves to the top or bottom boundary, those signals (both reversal and continuation) are going to be stronger than elsewhere.

Resistance and Support

The foundation of trade timing is going to be found in resistance and support. In traditional definitions, these are the top and bottom price levels where trading occurs. The trading range resides between resistance and support, and continues until there is a breakout, either above or below.

The value of observing the trading range residing in between resistance and support is not only useful in determining the likelihood of price movement outside of that range. These borders also define the level of volatility in a stock's price. Risk itself is defined as the degree of volatility in price. A lower degree of certainty translates to greater risk. Resistance and support will vary based on the fundamentals, as well as on recent trends in historical volatility. As a result, the defined trading range clearly marked by resistance and support identifies volatility itself.

The traditional resistance and support levels can be observed. These lines may rise or fall, or they may move sideways. An example is shown in Fig. 4.1.

In the first section of the chart, a strong bullish trend is defined clearly by the narrow channel of price in between resistance and support. The end of the trend is found in the bearish reversal candlestick, the three inside down. A successful breakout is marked at this spot.

The breakout takes price down to a new trading range, between resistance at $164 per share and support at $155. This is tested immediately with the breakout in early March, but it fails, and price retraces back into the newly established range.

Fig. 4.1 Resistance and support

This example reveals the strength of resistance and support as signals to clarify the trend and price direction. The channels created by resistance and support also define the direction of the trend. In the example, a strong bullish trend is defined with a narrow, advancing channel, and in the last section, a consolidation trend is defined by sideways-trending resistance and support.

Bollinger Bands

The levels of resistance and support can be more clearly observed with the use of a key technical signal, Bollinger Bands. This consists of three bands: middle, upper and lower. The middle band is a 20-day simple MA of price.

Upper and lower bands are each two standard deviations removed from the middle band. Standard deviation is a statistical calculation that makes historical volatility visual. This is of great value to options traders, because volatility defines risk, and as it grows or shrinks, the timing of trades is vastly improved. Bollinger Bands provides not only a dynamic version of resistance and support but also a measurement of the risk trend:

> In finance, standard deviation is a statistical measurement; when applied to the annual rate of return of an investment, it sheds light on the historical volatility of that investment. The greater the standard deviation of a security, the greater the variance between each price and the mean, indicating a larger price range. For example, a volatile stock has a high standard deviation, while the deviation of a stable blue-chip stock is usually rather low.[3]

The traditional straight line of resistance and support is effectively improved by replacement with Bollinger Bands. Figure 4.2 is a new version of the previous chart with this change shown. It reveals the advantages of Bollinger Bands.

The same channels and breakouts are visible with this chart as on the previous one. However, breakouts can be observed not only as movements outside of identified resistance or support, but also outside of the two standard deviations. When price moves above the upper band or below the lower band, the expectation for a fast correction is apparent. In most cases, the opposite direction is established rapidly.

Another advantage is revealed in the analysis of resistance and support, through the development of clear channels and trends. In an uptrend, the upper band acts as dynamic resistance and the middle band becomes support, and in a downtrend, the middle band becomes declining resistance and the lower band becomes support. An examination of the chart with these observations in mind reveals the value of Bollinger Bands as tests of current trends.

Fig. 4.2 Bollinger Bands

Like the traditional straight-line forms of resistance and support, Bollinger Bands presents a version of the trading range, but is more dynamic. However, they do not provide definite answers to the timing puzzle, but more of a relative value test:

> Trading bands are one of the most powerful concepts available to the technically based investor, but they do not, as is commonly believed, give absolute buy and sell signals based on price touching the bands. What they do is answer the perennial question of whether prices are high or low on a relative basis. Armed with this information, an intelligent investor can make buy and sell decisions by using indicators to confirm price action.[4]

T-Line

Yet another change needs to be added to the chart for analysis of trading ranges and reversals. The t-line is an eight-day exponential MA of price. It sets up easily observed changes in price direction.

The t-line identifies changes in price direction, specifically swing trades. Because this is only an eight-day average, its value is limited but as a confirming signal, it increases confidence when a reversal is observed. Figure 4.3 shows how adding the t-line to Bollinger Bands strengthens the resistance and support trend and identifies reversals.

The "rule" for the t-line is that when price crosses and closes above the line for two or more days, the price trend turns bullish, and when it crosses below the t-line and closes there for two or more days, the price trend turns bearish.

Fig. 4.3 Bollinger Bands and the t-line

As a confirming signal for other reversal indicators, the t-line is powerful. However, it also shows up at points of retracement and could mislead you by implying that a new trend has developed. For example, on the chart, retracement occurred on November 10 and 13 (a Friday and Monday), and as the chart shows, this was not reversal. The same thing happened on February 23 and 26.

The t-line is an extremely short-term indicator, but at points of true reversal, it is a strong confirming signal. For example, at the two strongest reversal points on this chart, highlighted on January 30–31 and March 14–15, the t-line crossed the Bollinger middle band. When the t-line moves below the middle band (as it did in January), it confirms a bearish reversal. When it crosses above the middle band, as it did in March, it points to a likely bullish reversal.

When the t-line is added to Bollinger Bands, it works in conjunction with the middle band to identify support (in bullish moves) or resistance (in bearish moves); however, crossover between t-line and middle band adds an additional dimension to the analysis. This powerful combined analytical tool supports a contention often stated among technicians:

> One of the stock market technician's most prized tools is the chart of individual security price movements. The technician contends that certain price patterns recur frequently and that price direction subsequent to the formation of these patterns is predictable.[5]

Even so, the predictive value of any technical signal is viewed with skepticism in academia, and among some traders who believe in the random walk hypothesis (RWH). Analysis of many signal patterns over a period reveals that some signals are highly reliable for predicting *likely* price movement, and among the most predictable is the combination of Bollinger Bands with crossover signals, including the t-line and other MAs.

Gaps and Tops or Bottoms

Another popular set of reversal signals occur often and are recognized easily. These include gaps as well as tops or bottoms; when both types appear together, the reversal indication is exceptionally strong. When they appear together *and* at the point of resistance or support, they get very close to 100 percent confidence in reversal happening next.

Gaps occur often on stock charts. They are so frequent that, by themselves, gaps do not provide reliable signals. However, gaps are found in many of the popular technical signals and define their importance. The inclusion of gaps as part of a candlestick reversal, for example, is easily quantified by the nature of the gap itself. The larger the gap, the stronger the signal.

Despite the belief among many traders that gaps are exceptions to an otherwise orderly price pattern, an examination of a stock chart proves that they are not by any means an exception. However, recognizing types beyond *common gaps* helps to add strength to likely reversal.

A *runaway gap* is seen when price is moving strongly in one direction. The greater the momentum seen in runaway gaps, the stronger a reversal is likely to be when it does appear. An *exhaustion gap* appears at the top of a trend right before reversal and is particularly compelling when it represents the last entry in a series of runaway gaps. A *breakaway gap* is significant, because it moves price above resistance or below support. If accompanying confirmation signals of reversal are found, the likely indication is a retreat into the previous range. If a continuation signal and confirmation are found, the breakaway gap is the strongest evidence of a successful breakout above or below the current range.

When gaps appear at mid-range, they probably do not mean much. A reversal is most likely when it consists of a breakaway gap at the point of resistance or support. When gaps are accompanied with tops (the last point in the current trend, consisting of two or more topping days) or bottoms (the same pattern at the bottom), the gaps confirm likely reversal. Double (or triple) tops and bottoms are strong reversal signals, so the occurrence of these last legs in the trend, along with breakaway gaps, is among the strongest signals on a stock chart.

A study of almost any stock chart reveals a high volume of gaps and double (or triple) tops and bottoms. For example, Fig. 4.4 identifies several strong and high-momentum short-term trends, each market with forms and combinations

Fig. 4.4 Gaps and tops or bottoms

of gaps and tops or bottoms. The longest trend on this chart lasted two months, from November to January. It was characterized by several runaway gaps, which served as an early warning sign that the trend would be likely to end soon. The exhaustion gap was easily spotted because the gap was large and, a few days later, confirmed the end of the trend with a double top. The final consolidation trend concluded with a strong breakaway gap, taking price above the short-term resistance and followed by strong upward momentum.

Chart analysis reveals patterns such as these for past price activity. The more study of past patterns a trader executes, the more likely that reversal and continuation patterns will be recognized as they emerge.

Rounded Tops or Bottoms and Island Reversals

Like the double top and double bottom formation are other reversal signals. These appear at the top of an uptrend and anticipate a downtrend, or at the bottom of a downtrend, anticipating a reversal and uptrend.

The *rounded top* and *rounded bottom* form a rounding shape and, while more difficult to spot than the double top or bottom, are strong reversal signals. An example of the rounded top reversal is shown in Fig. 4.5.

In this chart, three rounded top patterns clearly mark the reversal points of previous uptrends. A similar pattern is found in rounded bottoms, as shown in Fig. 4.6.

58   M. C. Thomsett

Fig. 4.5 Rounded tops

Fig. 4.6 Rounded bottoms

In this chart, the patterns mark the conclusion of short-term downtrends and turning points, followed by short-term uptrends.

In the *island reversal* (also called *island cluster*), you find an exceptionally strong reversal signal. It is marked by gaps on either side and a short-term period of trades on an "island" either above or below the established trading range. Figure 4.7 shows how strongly these patterns anticipate strong reversal.

Fig. 4.7 Island reversals

Candlestick Reversal

The Japanese candlestick has become the chart pattern of choice, the default in most charting services. However, even though traders may understand the basic significance of the candlestick session, the signals and their strength are not well understood.

Most traders understand that a session with a white (or clear) real body is a session moving upward, and that the opening price is at the bottom of the real bottom with the closing price at the top. The extensions above and below, called shadows or wicks, represent the session's trading range above and below the open-to-close price levels.

What is less understood is the various patterns that evolve in single sessions, double sessions or three consecutive sessions. Numerous strong reversals are found among the many candlesticks and can aid in identification of likely reversal timing. As with all reversal signals, confirmation should be found in Western indicators, other candlesticks, volume signals, momentum oscillators and MAs before entering or exiting a trade.

For example, Fig. 4.8 highlights several candlestick reversal and continuation signals. This reveals the extent of signals emerging within normal swing trades; however, before acting on any signals, confirmation is essential.

The reversals on this chart consist of both two-session and three-session signals. Some chart analysts claim that three-session signals are stronger than the two-session ones, but "strength" relies more on proximity (to resistance or support) and whether a confirming signal is also located.

Fig. 4.8 Candlestick reversal signals

The first bullish signal led to a strong movement in price, but the only confirmation consisted of several strong price gaps as price rose. The bearish engulfing at the top of the trend was confirmed by the three inside down signal. The bullish harami predicted an uptrend, and this occurred, but only briefly. Following this uptrend, the three black crows—an especially strong bearish signal—led to a two-week decline. The final bullish harami was not a strong signal and was not confirmed. By the conclusion of the chart, price appeared to have moved into a consolidation period.

Candlestick Continuation

Beyond reversal, candlesticks also provide confirmation signals that help identify when a current trend has not yet exhausted. Confirmation also exists in the form of Western signals, notably triangles and wedges. These are not the most reliable signals, so candlestick continuation tends to provide more dependable signaling, assuming confirmation is also found. However, continuation patterns are more difficult to find than reversals.

The chart in Fig. 4.9 provides two examples. Following a long period of consolidation, price made a strong move upward, then downward. This marked a period of volatility. The bearish thrusting lines were a forecast of continued downward pressure. Following a brief upward movement, price did decline. Finally, the upside gap filled predicted continued bullish movement which, by the conclusion of the chart, had not yet occurred.

Timing with Well-Selected Technical Signals   61

Fig. 4.9 Candlestick continuation signals

Continuation signals are useful for managing volatility. In opening short positions as part of an installment strategy, recognizing when price is approaching peaks and valleys within the current range helps time short entry and exit to produce consistent short-term profits.

Volume Indicators

Beyond price indicators, several volume signals are useful in confirming reversal or continuation. Among the volume signals used by technicians are on balance volume (OBV), money flow index (MFI), accumulation/distribution (A/D) and more. However, perhaps the most revealing and easily recognized volume indicator is the spike.

A spike is an exceptionally high-volume day (or two or three). To count as a spike, the daily volume should return to more typical levels immediately after the spike is seen. The spike is a strong confirming indicator of price reversal.

An example is shown in Fig. 4.10.

The strength of the volume spike is evident in this example. After a period of five months of sideways price movement, a large price gap and long black candle—both bearish—identified a strong breakout. Confirming this was the volume spike, which was at least four times higher than previous volume levels. It then returned to more typical levels after the gap and long black session was concluded.

Fig. 4.10 Volume spike

The volume spike provides exceptional confirmation for reversals in price. However, using volume indicators for historical comparisons and even for current price trends is of limited value. For confirmation purposes, the study of volume is less clear in terms of value than price-specific indicators:

> Financial academics and practitioners have long recognized that past trading volume may provide valuable information about a security. However, there is little agreement on how volume information should be handled and interpreted. Even less is known about how past trading volume interacts with past returns in the prediction of future stock returns.[6]

Momentum Oscillators

Yet another source of reversal and confirmation is a series of momentum oscillators. Momentum does not measure the direction of price movement, only its speed and strength. Numerous oscillators are used in technical analysis, including stochastics and moving average convergence/divergence (MACD). However, the easiest to track and understand is relative strength index (RSI).

This measures the balance between higher and lower closing prices and sets up an index between 0 and 100, over a 14-session MA. When the index value

Fig. 4.11 Relative strength index (RSI)

moves above 70, the stock is identified as overbought, and when it moves below 30, it is oversold. By itself, RSI may not provide reliable reversal timing signals, and there have been cases of price remaining above 70 or below 30 for an extended period. However, as a confirming indicator, it is a useful test for timing of reversal entry or exit.

An example of RSI is shown in Fig. 4.11. Then momentum oscillator predicts turning points once trends approach their exhaustion point.

The strong uptrend began in November and lasted through the end of January. However, RSI moved into overbought at the beginning of January, four weeks before the trend reversed. On the downside, price dropped 12 points very quickly. However, RSI moved to oversold just as the downtrend ended. This indicated that the price was likely to reverse once more and move to the upside. This occurred, but it took two months for a reversal to begin.

This points out that RSI can anticipate reversals, but the timing is questionable. In these examples, a considerable delay between signal and response was evident. RSI and other momentum oscillators identify the likely price levels for reversal, but the precise timing for reversal to occur is more difficult. Therefore, momentum works best as a confirming indicator and should not be used by itself to time entry or exit.

Moving Averages

A final source for signals is the MA. A single MA is merely a lagging indicator of price. However, using two MA lines with different time periods, while still lagging indicators, sets up a method to anticipate price movement.

A popular combination is a 50-day and 200-day MA. The 50-day tends to be more responsive to price behavior, so the use of both MA lines can provide some signals of likely price trends. In a chart using MA lines, several possible signals can be useful in timing short-term entry and exit. These include crossover and divergence trends.

A chart with 50 MA and 200 MA is shown in Fig. 4.12.

The darker line represents a 200 MA and the lighter line is the 50 MA. In the first portion of the chart, price was above both averages, but it crossed below in early February. This was a bearish signal. It was confirmed when the 50 MA crossed below the 200 MA on March 20. This version of crossover is equally bearish.

Even though these are lagging indicators, the interaction of one MA to the other and the movement of price in relation to the MA lines are excellent confirming signals. When the crossover is to the upside, the opposite indication develops. Crossover above the MA lines is a bullish signal, and crossover of the 50 MA above the 200 MA is also bullish.

The dozens of possible reversal and continuation signals make technical analysis complex. However, by focusing on a short list of highly reliable signals and then seeking equally reliable confirmation improve entry and exit

Fig. 4.12 Moving averages

timing significantly. This is an essential skill for identifying trading decisions for the short options used to pay for longer term long options within the installment strategy.

The first of two general installment strategies is the *risk hedge,* combining a long LEAPS put with short-term short options trades. This hedging strategy is appropriate for investors who own shares of stock and want to eliminate market risk in the event of a price decline. A LEAPS put, once paid down to a zero basis, eliminates risk below the put's strike.

Notes

1. Levy, R. (1966). Conceptual foundations of technical analysis. *Financial Analysts Journal,* Volume 22, No. 4, pp. 83–89.
2. Blume, L., Easley, D., & O'Hara, M. (1994). Market statistics and technical analysis: The role of volume. *The Journal of Finance,* Volume 49, No. 1, pp. 153–181.
3. www.investopedia.com/terms/s/standarddeviation.asp, retrieved April 19, 2018.
4. Bollinger, J. (January 1992) Using Bollinger Bands. *Stocks & Commodities,* Volume 10, No. 2, pp. 47–51.
5. Levy, R. A. (1971). The predictive significance of five-point chart patterns. *The Journal of Business,* Volume 44, No. 3, pp. 316–323.
6. Lee, C. & Swaminathan, B. (October 2000). Price momentum and trading volume. *The Journal of Finance,* Volume LV, No. 5, pp. 2017–2069.

5

Long-Term Market Risk Elimination

The risk hedge is a simple idea at first glance. However, there are five possible outcomes, and these are explained later in this chapter. The essence of the strategy is that puts can be used to eliminate market risk in an equity position. This addresses the unending concern investors have: if I buy stock, how can I be sure its value will not decline?

Much of the literature on the topic of risk hedging points to the problems of creating a truly risk-free (perfect) hedge:

> To create and maintain a risk-free hedge by using movements in an asset as inherently unstable as options to offset movements in an asset as inherently unstable as stock, requires investors to rebalance these positions often enough to adequately approximate a risk-free hedge, but not so often as to generate economically infeasible transaction costs. Conceivably, no such "middle" strategy exists.[1]

This conclusion is outdated and does not consider the stability of the LEAPS options used in the risk hedge discussed in this chapter. The LEAPS was developed several years before this paper was published but did not come into popular use until the Internet made options trading affordable and practical. For example, the mention of transaction costs outdates the observation. Before the Internet was used for trading, these costs were high; today, transaction costs are so low that they are no longer an inhibiting factor in developing a risk hedge. The concern among investors about the safety of their capital is a valid and ongoing issue, but risk hedging is an effective method for eliminating market risk.

© The Author(s) 2018
M. C. Thomsett, *Options Installment Strategies*,
https://doi.org/10.1007/978-3-319-99864-0_5

Any time that you buy stock, you live with the risk that price per share will fall. In that event, you must wait out a reversal, hoping price will return to your basis and eventually move higher. Or, in the alternative, you must sell shares, take the loss and try again with another company's stock.

Both outcomes are unsatisfactory. There is a tendency among some investors to assume that the price per share paid at the time an equity position is entered is a "starting point," the "zero" price, and that from that purchase date, price will rise. This is untrue, of course. Price may either rise or fall. Proponents of the random walk hypothesis (RWH) contend that price movement is not predictable, and there is a 50 percent chance of movement in either direction. Whereas technicians contend that knowledge of past price behavior helps to predict short-term price activity, proponents of RWH "maintain that the conflicting actions of the many traders tend to neutralize any systematic price behavior, and thus actual prices wander randomly about their economic value."[2]

With the debate unsettled between the schools of random walk and technical analysis, every investor needs to determine how reliable technical signals might be, and whether a risk hedge is useful in timing of trades. RWH is partially true, but not exclusively so. In fact, it is possible to increase your favorable odds with careful selection of companies based on strong fundamentals, and with timing of trade entry and exit.

To solve the problem of a decline in stock price after purchase, other solutions are needed. This chapter demonstrates that this risk can be completely defeated with the *risk hedge* created with the installment put.

The Nature of Underlying Risk

Most investors understand risk at least on one level. The value of equity positions can decline, and might take weeks or months to recover, if it ever recovers at all. This basic market risk is the most obvious of risks, but it is not the entire story. Equally profound in its effect on decisions to place capital at risk is the intangible question of whether investors believe the market can be judged fairly:

> The decision to invest in stocks requires not only an assessment of the risk-return trade-off given the existing data, but also an act of faith (trust) that the data in our possession are reliable and that the overall system is fair ... [Investors] need to have trust in the fairness of the game and kin the reliability of the numbers to invest in it.[3]

This summarizes the problem of risk for investors. It points out that there must be some consistent method for quantifying risk in both equity and options trades. The most reliable method is a multi-year analysis of fundamentals, not in isolation but as parts of the whole. Fundamental selection of a company is a sensible starting position for any options trading program. Unfortunately, many options traders focus solely on identification of advantageous options trades and often do not care about the underlying security. This is a mistake. Starting with strong fundamentals and limiting the list of potential underlying securities on which options will be traded makes sense.

The risk hedge underscores the importance of company selection as a first step. Because it is designed to eliminate market risk in a position currently owned, a fair assumption is that you want to hold shares in your portfolio. However, the question must be asked: how did you choose that company? If you did not qualify the company as a starting point, why continue to own shares? Hedging with options is effective, but it also makes sense to improve likely outcomes by restricting equity positions to exceptional companies and their stock.

At least four other types of risks should be understood by anyone considering an installment trade for risk hedging:

1. Trading an Ill-Timed Equity Position The risk of poor timing is well known to most investors. Buying shares at a price peak, only to witness a reversal and decline, is a common experience. On the other end of a trade, selling at a price bottom and then seeing price rise after the sale is a frustrating experience. These are *timing* problems, and they can be avoided by understanding the nature of emotions and the role they play in how trading takes place.

Buying at the top of a price trend often results from the desire to be in a position and to not miss out on more price appreciation. However, an investor who pays attention to the technical signals can recognize when a trend is approaching its exhaustion point. At this point, a growing number of investors take up positions, which is the worst timing for entering a long equity position.

Selling at the bottom is equally ill timed. It occurs when investors fear further declines and want to exit before losing more capital. In the same way that buying at the top is ill advised, selling at the bottom makes no more sense. The practice of ill timing may be termed, "Buy high, sell low." This is the opposite of the wisdom in the advice: "Buy low, sell high."

2. Confirmation Bias People tend to see what they want, which is termed confirmation bias, defined as "the tendency to search for, interpret, favor, and recall information in a way that confirms our pre-existing beliefs."[4]

This tendency can do great harm to investors and traders. For example, a trader believes a company is a "good investment," so among the fundamental indicators checked, some are positive, so these provide the basis to buy. But some others are very negative. Under the theory of confirmation bias, the trader ignores the negative signs and proceeds with a trade.

The solution is to develop fundamental and technical criteria for stock selection and apply these criteria to all candidates. Only enter an equity trade on those companies meeting the high standards. Chapter 3 provided a short list of valuable fundamentals worth checking, and Chap. 4 did the same for technical tests.

Applying these tests defeats confirmation bias and allows you to select an equity position based on fundamental and technical strength rather than intuition or impulse.

3. Unexpected Events There is no way to escape the impact of unexpected events in the qualification of a company or its stock value. These include earnings surprises, changed guidance, altered analysts' opinions and announcements of mergers or acquisitions.

Unexpected events may be factual or only rumor-based. It is impossible to know in the moment which "fact" is true and which is false; but a long-term tendency is for sudden changes in pricing to adjust and revert into a previously established range. The market tends to overreact in the short term to all unexpected news, and a sudden move in price is likely to be temporary. For swing traders, this sudden overreaction presents an opportunity to make a contrarian trade based on a belief that the price move is temporary.

An exception to this observation is what happens after one company announces the acquisition of another. If the offered price is higher than the current price of the company being acquired, it is reasonable to expect price to move close to that higher price. Assuming the deal goes through, that offer price will normalize. However, if the deal falls through or is challenged by the Federal Trade Commission (FTC), price is likely to move back to its previous level, and perhaps lower.

4. Ignoring the Fundamentals as Criteria for Selection Traders are prone to emotional responses to market movement. This is a significant risk for those considering an installment risk hedge. If a stock is purchased and then hedged with options, the purpose is to anticipate and prevent market risk from affecting value. However, this does not offset a decision made on the wrong criteria, namely the fundamentals.

A starting point in selection of stock should be the fundamentals, and only a few companies meet the highest standards (including dividend per share, dividend yield, price/earnings (P/E) ratio ranges, revenue, earnings, net return and long-term debt to total capitalization ratio). Because only a small number of companies meet these high standards, the list of candidates can be narrowed down to only a few.

The risk hedge should not be viewed as an excuse for picking fundamentally weak companies. The assumption about the risk hedge is that a company's stock is first selected due to strong fundamentals. Then the risk hedge is entered to protect the position in the event the stock price declines below the long put's strike. A belief that the fundamentals do not matter because the risk hedge protects against market risk overlooks the importance of investing in strong companies that (a) pay exceptional dividends, (b) maintain reasonable stock price levels, (c) yield growing (not shrinking) revenue and earnings and (d) control levels of long-term debt capitalization. In other words, the risk hedge protects against market risk, but in the long term, financially stable and strong investments are requisites for success.

The Risk Hedge with Long Puts

The risk hedge strategy contains three segments. First is the selection of a company as a potential investment. Once qualified, its stock is purchased. For example, assume that a company meets all the fundamental criteria previously described, so an investor buys 100 shares.

The second segment is purchase of a LEAPS put. This long put should be set at a strike close to the purchase price per share. This insurance put offsets risk below the strike. This means that by expiration, if the stock price is lower than the put's strike, the value of the put will match the number of points of decline in the stock. For example, if the strike is 50 and stock declines to $44 per share, intrinsic value in the put will be 6 ($600), offsetting the stock price decline. The problem with the trade to this point is that the cost of the put reduces the insurance. Given the example of a 6-point decline, if the put cost 4 ($400), the risk hedge provides only two points of hedged value. The insurance put (protective put) offers a solution as well as a problem when considered by itself. This is the combination of reduced market risk with a reduction in potential gains due to the cost of insurance:

Purchasing a put on stock in its own portfolio entitles a institution to sell the stock at a specific price until a certain date. The institution thus reduces its gain from any possible price rise by the premium paid for the put. On the other hand, it is protected against price declines. Thus purchase of a protective put entails less risk and less expected return than purchase of stock alone.[5]

The expected shortfall caused by the need to pay for the put is addressed by the third segment of the installment-based risk hedge. In this segment, the investor sells a series of extremely short-term puts or calls. Ideally, expiration should take place in one week or, at the most, two weeks. This is the period during which time decay is at its most accelerated. The reason for picking short-term short options is to exploit time decay and, over the entire period until the LEAPS expiration, to pay for that long position with profits from these short positions.

The one-week expiration is most advantageous. Because a short position is open, a trader desires rapid decline in the premium value. A "sell to open" is followed by a "buy to close" trade, so the more rapidly decline occurs, the greater this advantage. The Friday before expiration (exactly one week away) is the best time for opening the short position. Over the weekend, three calendar days pass but only one trading day. However, time decay occurs on every day, including days when the market is closed. As a result, the average option value changes advantageously: "During the weekend that precedes expiration, an option contract loses 32.8% of its remaining time."[6]

All short positions should be opened with a buffer zone between strike and current price. This ensures that unfavorable underlying movement will not necessarily move the exposed short position in the money. For short puts, the strike should be buffered below current price. For short calls, the strike should be higher.

The Trade: Long-Term Long Put and Short-Term Short Positions

If the short-term short calls and puts are well managed and timed, they are expected to pay for the long-term LEAPS put. In the ideal risk hedge, this is precisely what occurs. But the trade does not always turn out as expected. Several events may affect the risk hedge.

First, the long put could increase in value. When this occurs, the risk hedge can be closed at a profit. Any interim short option profits have been realized, but now the long put can also be closed at a profit. If an investor decides to take profits, it then becomes possible to enter a new risk hedge, potentially with a different strike. If the put has gained value, it means the underlying price declined, so selection of a new strike should take into consideration the condition of underlying stock and the degree to which this is adjusted by profits from both long put and short options. The trader may also decide to escape the equity position and exercise the long put, selling shares at the strike. However, this only makes sense if the net profit from exercise exceeds the cost of the long put, and this probably will not be possible. Selling stock early does not make sense, considering that the risk hedge is intact.

Second, an open short position could move in the money, requiring a roll forward or close at a loss. When a short put or call moves in the money, it presents a problem. This means that the stock price is higher than a call's strike or lower than a put's strike and—because these are short-term options—exercise is a possibility. The short position must be rolled forward (closed at a loss and replaced by a later expiring position) or closed at a loss. The forward roll is easily executed, but this extends the time a position is open. The ideal trade involves opening and closing options every week when possible and taking profits. Rolling forward defers the profit to a later date. Taking a loss often makes more sense and is a reality as part of the risk hedge, if overall outcomes are profitable enough to pay for the long put.

Third, if the in-the-money short position is not managed, it will be exercised. This is the worst outcome of all, if you do not want your 100 shares called away (with exercise of a short call) or another 100 shares put to you (with exercise of a short put). Both outcomes are undesirable in the risk hedge. However, if shares are called away at a profit, it is not a dire result. However, it leaves you with a long-term put that still needs to be paid for with short options, or eventually closed. If a short put is exercised, you acquire an additional 100 shares at the strike. Some investors will just sell these shares and take a loss; others will view this as an opportunity. If long-term prospects for the company's shares are still viewed favorably, this doubles the equity position and may lead the trader to increase the risk hedge as well. That would mean buying a second put and from that point forward, selling two options each week to offset two long puts protecting 200 shares.

For example, 100 shares of Verizon (VZ) were purchased on February 9, 2018. The price per share was $50.50 and with trading fees, the total paid was $5055. By April 13, the price had not moved significantly and the decision was made to begin a risk hedge to protect share price. The selected strike was $47 per share.

The first step was to purchase a LEAPS put at the 47 strike. The January 2019 47 strike was available at an ask price of 3.80 and one put was purchased at a total cost of $385.

Table 5.1 Risk hedge, Verizon

	Purchase		Sale		
Description of the trade	Date	Amount ($)	Date	Amount ($)	Profit ($)
1 call, Apr 13, 47 strike, bid 0.94	4/9/18	44	4/5/18	89	45
1 put, Apr 13, 47 strike, bid 0.45	4/11/18	23	4/5/18	40	17
1 put, Apr 20, 47 strike, bid 0.40	4/16/18	14	4/5/18	35	21
2 calls, May 4, 48.50 strike, bid 2.46	5/1/18	204	4/27/18	486	282
2 calls, May 11, 47 strike, bid 0.39	5/9/18	13	5/9/18	72	59
2 puts, May 25, 48 strike, bid 0.60	5/21/18	78	5/16/18	114	36
2 puts, May 25, 48.50 strike, bid 0.63	5/21/18	82	5/21/18	120	38
2 puts, May 25, 49 strike, bid 0.68	5/23/18	66	5/18/18	130	64
2 puts, Jun 1, 49 strike, bid 0.46	5/31/18	190	5/23/18	86	−104
2 puts, Jun 8, 48.50 strike, bid 0.68	6/7/18	21	5/31/18	130	109
Total		735		1302	567
1 long put, 47 strike, ask 3.80, 1/18/19	4/4/18	385			−385
Net profit (56 days)		1120		1302	182

Source: Net trades executed by the author

The second step was to open a series of short trades (either call or put) to pay for the LEAPS put. From the time the LEAPS was opened on April 4, until expiration of the following January 19, there were 352 days to go. The focus on extremely short-term expiration would ensure maximum exploitation of time decay. A series of ten short trades were opened and closed between April and June 2018. In two months, the LEAPS put was more than paid for, and a summary of all trades is provided in Table 5.1.

The trades mostly spanned 4 or 5 days; the longest one was 11 days. Overall, profits from the three short calls and seven short puts were $567, not only paying for the LEAPS put but exceeding the cost by $182.

With the January 2019 put at a zero basis after the short option offsets, the 100 shares of Verizon were protected below the strike of 47. The original cost per share had been $50.50 per share, so this strike is $350 under the original basis. This is reduced by the $182 net profits shown on the table, for a net of only $168 maximum potential loss.

As of June 8—only two months after the risk hedge was opened—the cost of the LEAPS put was completely covered by short-term options trades. At this point, with seven months remaining before expiration of the LEAPS put, generating an additional $168 in profits will eliminate the points between original basis and the long put's strike.

The complete elimination of market risk in the 100 shares was accomplished in only 56 days.

Calculating the Point of Risk Elimination

Any investor entering a risk hedge should calculate the point at which risk is eliminated. This means that the long put has been paid for and a perfect hedge is created. A "perfect hedge" is one that eliminates market risk in another position, and this is exactly what the risk hedge is designed to accomplish.

To calculate the required frequency of profit generation, a first short trade is first executed. Assuming the same level of weekly profits can be generated, you determine how many short trades must be entered to pay for the long put. Dividing the number of days by the number of required trades, you next identify how often a trade must be executed.

For example, you open a LEAPS long put expiring in 202 days and pay a total of $2285. At the same time, you sell a short put for 50 and receive a net of $145 (premium minus trading fee of $5). The trade is opened the Friday before expiration and closed the following Thursday for $35. Net profit is $110 on this short trade.

How many times would a similar trade have to be executed to pay for the long put? To determine this, divide the net cost of the long put by the profit from the short put:

$$\$2285 \div \$110 = 21 \text{ (rounded up)}$$

If you generate $110 net profit consistently, you will need to execute a similar trade 21 times between now and expiration of the long put. That will pay for the long put. How often do you need to enter and exit a similar trade? To determine, divide the number of days until expiration of the long put by the number of times you need to execute a short trade:

How practical is this? Can you enter 21 trades, each yielding about $110, in 202 days? Dividing the total days by the number of required trades, you determine the number of days each trade needs to involve:

$$202 \text{ days} \div 21 \text{ trades} = 10 \text{ (rounded up)}$$

You need to execute similar trades every ten days. If you open a position on Friday prior to expiration and close it the following Thursday, repeating this every week, you will pay for the long put in a six-day series of trading. This allows some room for rolling forward, and for short positions yielding less than the estimated $110 profit. Traders may also employ creative positions such as ratio write short calls or ratio short put positions, and to exploit underlying price movement creating advantageous trading situations. For example, a big move following an earnings surprise creates an opportunity to enter a ratio position and increase profits based on observations about price behavior, proximity of underlying price to resistance or support and high-volatility periods when option premium is relatively rich.

Going through this mathematical exercise is essential prior to entering a risk hedge. You need to be reasonably sure that the goal of paying for the long put is practical. If the requirement for frequency of profits from opening short options is too severe, the strategy will not work out. The only escape from this negative result would be early closure or exercise, but that should not be the basis for entering the trade. In the example above, a successful trade would have to be opened and closed every ten days. With the ideal time of seven days in mind, this would be likely to end up profitably. However, the point is that the more often a trade is needed, the more a setback will harm the strategy.

A solution to a marginal risk hedge may have to be to accept higher risks on the short side of the trade. For example, relying on variable ratio writes or covered strangles would double the potential profit assuming none of the positions move in the money.

In a *variable ratio write*, more calls are written than can be covered with stock. For example, executing a risk hedge with 300 shares could involve opening four calls. Three are covered by stock and the fourth is uncovered. Another way to look at this strategy is that the short calls are all 75 percent covered. Two strikes are involved. Two of the calls should be opened at the next strike above current price, and the remaining two at the next strike above. If the underlying price advances toward the lower strike, one or more of the four calls can be closed to avoid exposure of the calls. The variable ratio write reduces the risk of the one-strike ratio write because avoiding exercise is made easier.

A *covered strangle* is a potentially profitable strategy when the underlying is range-bound. A consolidation trend may last for a considerable number of weeks, and this is the ideal timing for a two-part options strategy. A strangle is a variation of the straddle in which two different strikes are used. Both the short call and the short put are out of the money. A covered strangle is used when you also own shares of stock. For example, if you own 200 shares, a covered strangle can be designed in two ways. The first way is to open a covered call with a strike higher than the current value of the underlying, and an uncovered put with a strike below. This provides a buffer zone in the event of strong price movement in either direction. If the one-week period is used for this strategy, time decay is likely to make both sides profitable. In the second, more aggressive variety, if you own 200 shares, a covered strangle consists of two covered calls and two uncovered puts. This increases exposure on either side, but also expands the buffer zone. With more premium received for a total of four short positions, the risk hedge is more likely to end up profitably.

The expansion beyond matching short positions with increments of 100 shares increases market risk on the short side. However, combining covered calls with uncovered puts is a conservative strategy. Covered calls are protected by ownership of stock, so that assignment is satisfied by delivering shares. Uncovered puts have the same market risk as covered calls and, as a result, are also conservative trades. Unless the underlying is extremely volatile, the expanded covered strangle adds to cash income and pays for the long put much more rapidly.

Possible Outcomes

No matter how much you study the risk hedge, it does not always end up in the same way. There are five possible outcomes, and you need to be prepared for each:

1. Early Close Via Sale of the Long Put When you bought shares of the company, you had to believe that share value would rise over time. Otherwise, why put capital at risk? However, you also recognized that a drop in price was possible. If this occurred, you could sell the LEAPS put and take profits. A drop in the underlying price will result in an increase in the put's intrinsic value, so in theory, a paper loss in the stock is offset by profit in the short put.

In practice, this is not always possible. A long-term option is likely to experience an offset between intrinsic value and extrinsic value (implied volatility). The farther away expiration is, the more this offset is likely. For example, if the underlying price falls 6 points, you might see only a 4-point increase in the put's premium. This would consist of 6 points in intrinsic value, offset by a 2-point decline in the put's intrinsic value.

With this potentially unsatisfactory behavior in the LEAPS premium, selling the put early to offset losses is possible, but not guaranteed.

2. Exercise of a Short Position A second possibility is exercise of the short put, enabling you to sell 100 shares at the strike. At the time of this action, the underlying price would be lower than the strike, so the sale would be at a higher price per share than current value. The problem with this outcome is that the net profit in the stock (difference between strike and current value) might not be enough to offset the original cost of the put.

This problem arises because much of the premium (if not all of it) consists of time value. Consequently, the LEAPS put is expensive compared to likely intrinsic move. That expense might not cover the loss in stock, so like the first outcome, exercise is not likely to yield a net profit, especially early in the risk hedge process.

3. The Underlying Price Ends Up Above Strike When the underlying price has moved above the strike, which was the desired outcome when shares were purchased, the LEAPS put can be sold or allowed to expire. If the risk hedge has worked out, the net basis in the LEAPS put should be zero, since a series of sales would have reduced the net cost.

The insurance put created with the long put is a desirable feature in the risk hedge, because it eliminates all market risk (assuming the premium cost of the long put has been offset by premium income from short options). As a result, if there is any value remaining in the put, even a small value, selling the put sets up a profit because the basis is zero.

4. The Underlying Price Ends Up Below the Strike, and Exercise Results In this case, you may exercise the long put on the last trading day or before. This results in your selling 100 shares of the underlying at the strike, which will be higher than the current price per share. As a result, the hedge worked, and you avoided a net loss in shares of stock.

The outcome in this case is to eliminate all market risk and avoid a loss. There is no profit involved (unless short options exceeded the cost of the long put). However, the loss was avoided. Without the insurance put, the stock position would be at a paper loss, so exercising the long put fulfills the purpose of the insurance put.

5. The Underlying Price Ends Up Below the Strike, and the Long Put Is Sold At the last trading day, the put's value will consist of intrinsic value. Once time value has evaporated, a 6-point decline in the stock below the put's strike will be offset by a 6-point intrinsic premium in the put.

Selling the long put in this situation offsets the loss in stock, since the stock loss is equal to the put's net value. This action is appropriate when you want to continue owning stock even though its price per share decline during the period the risk hedge was in effect. At this point, a subsequent risk hedge could be created based on a different strike selected with current stock value in mind.

At this point, since there was no net loss in the stock, the new risk hedge can be developed with a lower strike. This is not truly a net loss, since dividends would have been earned during the entire period.

The risk hedge is not a complex strategy. It sets up an insurance put, which offsets underlying price decline with increase in the put's value. However, changes in long-term premium value will not yield the point-for-point offset expected from the insurance put until expiration is close. The second part is sell of a series of short-term short options, intended to reduce the LEAPS put value down to zero. Once this is accomplished, the risk hedge is made perfect. At the point of expiration, no net capital has been spent to set up the hedge, and any decline in the underlying below the strike is offset by intrinsic value in the long put.

Notes

1. Gilster, J. (1997). Option Pricing Theory: Is 'Risk-Free' Hedging Feasible? *Financial Management,* Volume 26, No. 1, pp. 91–105.
2. Fielitz, B. (1971). On the Random Walk Hypothesis. *The American Economist,* Volume 15, No. 1, pp. 105–107.
3. Guiso, L., Sapienza, P., & Zingales, L. (2008). Trusting the stock market. *The Journal of Finance,* Volume 63, No. 6, pp. 2557–2600.
4. Hobbs, R. (2017). *Create to learn: Introduction to digital literacy.* Hoboken NJ: Wiley-Blackwell, p. 161.
5. Pozen, R. (1978). The purchase of protective puts by financial institutions. *Financial Analysts Journal,* Volume 34, No. 4, pp. 47–60.
6. Augen, J. (2009). *Trading Options at Expiration.* Upper Saddle River NJ: Pearson Education, p. 41.

6

Long-Term Contingent Purchase

The LEAPS contract is opened like any other option. A long call expiring as far away as 30 months will be expensive because time value is high. For many traders, considering the purchase of an expensive call is unthinkable. For example, if a call costs $2500, it requires a 25-point move to the upside, just to break even and offset declining time value.

This concern is valid. However, when an installment purchase is organized and put into effect, the cost of the long call is reduced week after week as a series of puts and calls are sold. Due to the short time until expiration, time decay will be accelerated. Once the net basis in the long position has been reduced to zero, the trader can exercise the call and buy shares below current market value, or sell the call and take profits equal to intrinsic value.

Locking in the Future Price

The primary and immediate benefit to the installment purchase is locking in the future price. For many investors, the frustration of missed opportunities is a constant problem. Most active investors have considered buying shares in a company but have decided to "wait and see" what the price does. Then the price moves up, perhaps significantly, and the opportunity to invest at a bargain price has passed.

There is no way to know a future price, but several attributes of a company and its stock improve the chances for an accurate prediction. These include the following.

1. *Strong Fundamentals* The relationship between strong fundamentals and the prices of both stocks and options is clear: "Firms with low ratios of fundamentals (such as earning and book values) to market values are known to have systematically lower future stock returns."[1]

A company with low fundamental volatility is likely to experience strong price performance, and high fundamental volatility translates to high price volatility. For example, companies increasing dividends every year for ten years or more (while also reporting long-term debt level or declining) will tend to experience low price volatility and gradual increases in share price over time.

A comparison between two companies over a ten-year period makes this point. Table 6.1 shows a decade of results for revenue, earnings and net return (earnings divided by revenue). Kraft Heinz results were low volatility for the first five years; for the most recent five years, they were very volatile; and the last two years' results had a puzzling jump in net return. In comparison, Johnson & Johnson's results were consistent and did not reveal any fundamental volatility. The most recent year was the exception, but given the consistency prior to that, the results point out the differences.

2. *Low Volatility in Recent Price History* The price volatility is the outcome of fundamentals trends. Before entering an installment purchase trade, check the recent price volatility. The ideal candidate will be one reporting slow, steady growth in price over time. However, a retracement and price decline that you believe is a short-term adjustment that might point to excellent timing for locking in a future share price.

Table 6.1 Ten-year comparison

Fiscal year	Kraft Heinz (KHC) Revenue (millions $)	Earnings (millions $)	Return (%)	Johnson & Johnson (JNJ) Revenue (millions $)	Earnings (millions $)	Return (%)
2008	9886	845	8.5	63,747	12,949	20.3
2009	10,011	923	9.2	61,897	12,266	19.8
2010	10,495	865	8.2	61,587	13,334	21.7
2011	10,559	990	9.4	65,030	9672	14.9
2012	11,508	924	8.0	67,224	10,853	16.1
2013	11,030	−408	−3.7	71,312	13,831	19.4
2014	10,922	657	6.0	74,331	16,323	22.0
2015	18,338	634	3.5	70,074	15,409	22.0
2016	26,487	3632	14.8	71,890	16,540	23.0
2017	26,232	10,999	41.9	76,450	1300	1.7

Source: CFRA Stock Reports

Fig. 6.1 Three-year price charts, declining and advancing prices

In the previous example, Kraft Heinz was compared to Johnson & Johnson in terms of revenue, earnings and net return. To see how this trend carried over to price behavior, check Fig. 6.1.

As the fundamentals for Kraft Heinz became more volatile, the price dropped, and as the fundamentals for Johnson & Johnson continued strongly throughout most of the decade, price advanced.

3. Attractive Options Pricing Compared to Stock Price As a factor of volatility, the price of long-term options as call candidates, and the price of short-term calls to pay for the long calls, will vary considerably.

Table 6.2 Installment purchase comparisons

Company	5/3/18 close ($)	6/21/19 (413 days) Call	Ask	Cost ($)	5/11/18 (7 days) Call	Bid	Cost ($)	Number of times
AMZN	1572.08	1570	234.05	23,405	1572.50	22.50	2250	23,405 ÷ 2250 = 11
T	31.94	32	2.25	225	32	0.38	38	225 ÷ 38 = 6
CVX	126.01	125	10.70	1070	126	1.50	150	1070 ÷ 150 = 7

Substantial differences will be found among candidates for the installment purchase, in terms of the number of times a short option needs to be opened and closed to pay for a long option. Table 6.2 compares three different companies for long-term call ask prices and short-term call bid prices.

This table reveals that the highly volatile Amazon.com options would have to be opened and closed 11 times to pay for the long call. In comparison, AT&T at-the-money options would have to be opened and closed six times, and Chevron options seven times.

Low volatility has its benefits, as this table reveals. Higher option prices often are considered attractive by traders; but at least in the case of an installment purchase, the chances for succeeding in paying for the long call are improved by low volatility (as in the case of the second and third companies in the table).

The Risk Hedge for Future Purchase

The long-term purchase strategy is a risk hedge, but not the same as the risk hedge introduced in Chap. 5. The purchase-based risk hedge provides protection against declining stock prices in the future, while freezing the purchase price in the event the stock price advances. Risk factors are addressed by the hedge, a primary one being the risk that future stock prices will rise, and the trader did not take a position, either in stock or in options. Option risk factors cannot be ignored, however. It is a mistake to believe that hedges eliminate risk altogether: "The major *risk factors* of an option are the price of the underlying and its volatility"[2].

Hedging cannot completely remove risks in the underlying security. For example, if you buy shares of stock today and the price falls over the next year, you suffer a paper loss. You must wait for price to rebound or sell and take the loss. This is an unsatisfactory outcome for your investment dollars. As an alternative, buying a LEAPS call locks in today's price. If price drops, you have not committed capital beyond the LEAPS premium, and if price rises, you benefit from the appreciation through selling call or exercising the call. The problem remains, however, that a LEAPS call is expensive.

If the analysis stops there, it means you lose the premium if the underlying price declines. This is preferable to placing capital into the purchase of 100 shares, only to see its value decline. However, there is a solution to this. It involves the entire installment purchase in two parts: purchase of the LEAPS call and paying for that call by selling a series of short-term options.

The reduction of the LEAPS basis to zero means that in the event of a price decline in the underlying, nothing has been lost. However, if the price of the underlying advances, it means you can sell the LEAPS call at its intrinsic value or exercise the call and acquire 100 shares of stock. The benefit to this is that you gain a profit equal to the distance between the LEAPS strike and the current value of stock.

Figure 6.2 compares the charts of two companies, over a period of one year ending May 4, 2018. If a trader had opened an installment purchase of either of these, the outcomes would have been different by the end of the year.

Fig. 6.2 Outcomes of the installment purchase

A trader opening an installment purchase on General Mills probably would have picked a 55 strike. One year prior, this was the level of price for this company. However, one year later, the price had declined 12.5 points. Assuming a LEAPS call had been purchased and was paid for during the year, the trader would abandon the original plan to exercise the LEAPS call.

A trader opening the same strategy on Kohl's might have selected a 37.50 strike in the belief that the price would rise over a year. It traded sideways until November, and then price began rising strongly. By the end of the year, it had moved upward more than 25 points. At this price level, the trader has two choices just before expiration. Selling the LEAPS call for intrinsic value of more than 25 points yields a profit, or exercising the call allows the trader to buy 100 shares at the strike of 37.50. Assuming the LEAPS call had been paid for through the year, the zero net basis in the call makes either choice profitable.

These examples point out that you cannot know a year in advance whether a stock's price will rise or fall. This augments the value of the installment purchase strategy, assuming its net basis can be taken down to zero. The market and its components are a great uncertainty:

> Given the assumption of an efficient capital market, the pricing of the market portfolio at any point in time accurately reflects an equilibrium relationship between the market's consensus of risk and expected return.[3]

This is an attractive theory, but anyone who has tracked stock performance over time realizes that the market is chaotic and unpredictable. The best approach to stock selection must be based on strong fundamentals and timing of trades, whether stock purchase or options. The understanding that the markets are *not* efficient leads to the conclusion that using options to hedge makes sense, but also that intelligent stock selection is at the core of this strategy.

When a trader buys a long call without the offset of short options over time, the profitability of the speculative choice is affected by the original cost of the call. A price decline represents a total loss, and a price increase is a profit, but both outcomes are offset by the cost of the LEAPS call. Therefore, both sides—the long call and a series of short calls and puts—are needed.

Calculating the Point of Risk Elimination

Just as the risk hedge in the previous chapter must be analyzed before entry, the same is true for the installment purchase. The calculation of the point of risk elimination reveals whether the strategy makes sense, given a situation:

Long-Term Contingent Purchase

cost of the long LEAPS call and premium value of the short-term options to be written to pay down that initial premium.

The point is to determine how often a short position must be opened and closed, to generate profits. The goal is to pay the cost of the LEAPS call before expiration. That call may be taken down to a zero basis if enough short trades are generated, and after that you have the choice of selling the call and taking profits or exercising and buying shares. In either event, the net basis of the long call will be zero. However, if the analysis indicates that you will not be able to generate enough short trades, the installment strategy will not work.

For example, you open a long LEAPS call with a 35 strike, expiring in 182 days; you pay $1455. At the same time, you sell a seven-day short put and receive a net premium of 85 ($85). On the Tuesday before expiration, you buy to close the short put for $20, and book a net profit of $65. Assuming this is typical, the question is whether you can execute enough trades to pay down the call's basis from $1455 to zero. This first question is decided by dividing the long call's premium by the net profit on the short option:

$$\$1455 \div \$65 = 23 \ (\text{rounded up})$$

You need to execute 23 trades based on net profit of $65 to pay down the long call. How often would such a trade have to be executed? Divide the number of days to expiration by the number of times you need to execute a trade:

$$182 \div 23 = 8 \ (\text{rounded up})$$

You need to complete short trades every eight days, or slightly more than once per week. This seems to be a very close call. However, each trade, even if opened one week before expiration, does not have to be left open for the entire week. In the example given, a trade was opened on Friday and closed on Tuesday. That leaves 3 days to expiration, and a new trade can be opened the same day the first trade was closed. Time decay over 3 days will be accelerated, so chances of closing at a profit or allowing the position to expire worthless are very likely. At the same time, a subsequent one-week trade can be entered on expiration Friday for the following week.

This is a high-maintenance strategy. It demands constant watching. As a result, if you are not willing to enter such a marginal strategy, you can look elsewhere. For example, another situation presents itself. A 40-strike long call is currently priced at the ask price of 18.15 and can be opened for $1820. It expires in 210 days. The current 40 short put expiring in one week is priced at a bid of 1.10 and can be opened for a net of $105. You plan to let this option remain open until last trading day and closed close to zero or allowed to expire. Assuming you can earn a net profit of $90, how often would a similar trade have to be executed?

$$\$1820 \div \$105 = 18 \text{ (rounded up)}$$

You need to execute a similar trade 18 times to pay for the long call. How often would you need to execute a trade?

$$210 \div 18 = 12 \text{ (rounded up)}$$

You will need to complete a short trade every 12 days, closer to two weeks than one. This is far more flexible than the first example.

These examples summarize the process of analysis and comparison you must go through to decide whether the installment purchase strategy is practical. A 12-day requirement is more acceptable that an 8-day requirement, and leaves room for flexibility. For example, if a strategy does not work out and must be rolled forward, the 12-day average makes it possible to continue the strategy without running out of time.

Possible Outcomes

The installment purchase can end up in several ways:

1. Early Close Through Sell of the LEAPS Call If the underlying price advances enough to make the LEAPS call profitable, it can be closed, and profits taken. Although the purpose of the strategy is to lock in the price for possible purchase in the future, taking profits is one of several possibilities.

However, the fact that the LEAPS has become profitable does not mandate closing and taking profits. It only strengthens the strategy. The advancing price makes the initial call's strike even more attractive. The original intention in entering this strategy was to lock in the price of shares at the strike, so selling and taking profits is contrary to this purpose. Even so, it remains one possible outcome.

2. Exercise of the Short Option During the period between initiation of the strategy and expiration, a series of short options are opened and closed to pay for the LEAPS call. However, if any of those short options moves in the money, they could be exercised. This means that you lose money equal to the difference between the strike and current value (higher than strike for a short call or lower for a short put).

Exercise should be avoided, as it contradicts the purpose of the strategy. Use extremely short expiration terms, preferably one to two weeks, and close to take profits when they materialize. Using the LEAPS call to satisfy expiration is not usually profitable, since the longer term call will contain more time value than the exercised short position. Unless there is a big difference in the two strikes, this is not an acceptable conclusion to the strategy. For example, if your original call was purchased with a 35 strike and cost 8.50 points, you could use it to sell 100 shares at a 45 strike. This would set up a 10-point profit between the strikes (45 − 35), minus the 8.50 points, for a net of 1.50 profit (10 − 8.50).

Exercise of a put leads to 100 shares put to you at the strike. This could be advantageous if you want the shares, even though the cost will be higher than current market value. With 100 shares in your portfolio, you could continue with the installment purchase and add a long put for a risk hedge, setting up a spread or a straddle with the two LEAPS options.

3. The Underlying Price Moves Below the Call's Strike In this outcome, the LEAPS call eventually expires worthless. However, you can sell it for current value to get back some of its value. If the combined short option profits make up the difference, there is no loss. In fact, a declining underlying price would help you avoid a problem of paying for stock that later declined in value. The installment purchase strategy accomplishes two goals. First, it freezes the future purchase price at the strike. Second, in the event of a price decline, it helps you avoid ownership of stock purchased for a price above market value.

For example, Lockheed Martin was valued at $335.38 on March 2, 2018, when the contingent purchase was opened. At that time, a LEAPS call expiring September 21, 2018, was opened at a 335 strike, and a total of $2285 was paid. The number of days to expiration was 203 days. A total of ten short positions were opened, and profits on these totaled $2103. On May 1, the long-term call was valued at a bid price of 5.70 and was closed for a net of $565. This brought the total of credits to $2668, for a net profit of $388. The profit was 16.98 percent and, based on the long call being open for 60 days, annualized return of 101.30 percent:

$$\$388 \div \$2285 = 16.98\%$$
$$16.98 \div 60 \, \text{days} * 365 \, \text{days} = 101.30\%$$

The outcome of this installment purchase and its early close is summarized in Table 6.3.

The position was cancelled early because profits were possible, even though the share price declined from $335.38 at inception, down to $308.46 on May 1, a drop of $26.92 per share. The history during this period is summarized in Fig. 6.3.

Table 6.3 Contingent purchase plan, Lockheed Martin

	Purchase		Sale		
Description of the trade	Date	Amount ($)	Date	Amount ($)	Profit ($)
1335 Mar 2 put, bid 1.60	3/2/18	0	3/2/18	155	155
1332.50 Mar 9 put, bid 3.70	3/5/18	225	3/2/18	365	140
1340 Mar 9 put, bid 3.00	3/9/18	71	3/6/18	295	224
1335 Mar 29 put, bid 5.90	3/23/18	305	3/16/18	585	280
1335 Apr 6 put, bid 4.10	3/27/18	305	3/23/18	405	100
1335 Apr 13 put, bid 4.04	4/5/18	225	3/27/18	410	185
1342.50 Apr 20 call, bid 6.10	4/12/18	485	4/11/18	605	120
1 put Apr 20 345 strike, bid 2.30	4/17/18	100	4/16/18	225	125
1 call Apr 27 347.50 strike, bid 7.60	4/24/18	101	4/18/18	755	654
1 put Apr 27 325 strike, bid 1.65	4/27/18	40	4/26/18	160	120
Total		1857		3960	2103
Long call, 335 strike, 9/21/18	3/2/18	2285	5/1/18	570	−1715
Net profit (60 days)		4142		4530	388

Source: Net trades executed by the author

Fig. 6.3 Lockheed Martin

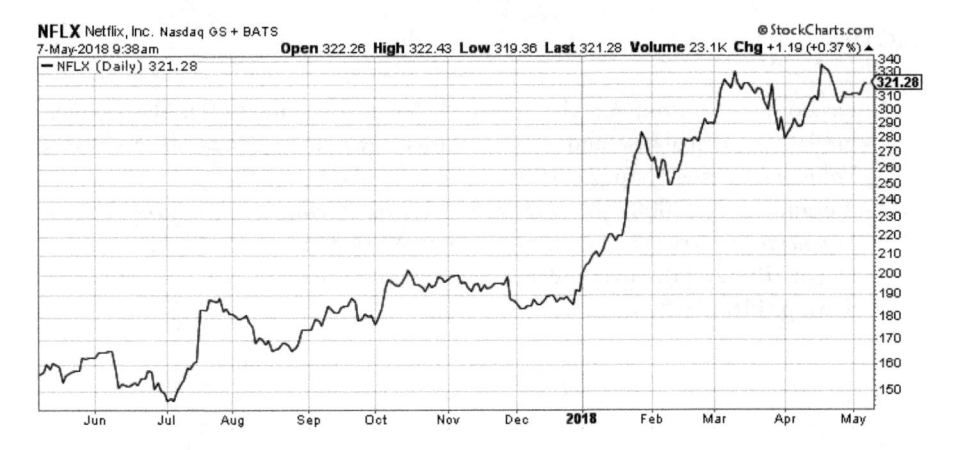

Fig. 6.4   Netflix

4. The Underlying Price of the Call Ends Up Above the Strike, and You Exercise If the price moves higher than the strike, you can exercise the long call and buy 100 shares at the strike—even if the price is substantially higher. For example, as of May 7, 2018, the price of Netflix (NFLX) had increased by over 104 percent over one year before. This is summarized in Fig. 6.4.

If you had opened a 160 strike LEAPS call expiring in one year in May 2017, it would have grown in value by 2018. It could be closed at a profit, or 100 shares could be purchased at $160, a profit of over $16,000 in the installment purchase. Because the basis in the call would be paid down to zero through the sale of short options over the year, the net basis is zero and the difference in price is all profit.

5. The Underlying Price Ends Up Above the Strike, and You Sell the Call Given the same example as above, you could also decide to sell the call rather than exercising it. Because net basis is zero, your profit is equal to all the current value in the call. This includes 160 points of intrinsic value plus any time value remaining at the point it is closed.

These outcomes demonstrate that the installment purchase offers great potential for profits or, if the price moves down, of avoiding any loss. However, the risk exposure of the short options opened and closed over the life of the strategy poses a serious risk. There are many ways to reduce this risk, which are explained in the next chapter.

Notes

1. Dechow, P.; Hutton, A.; Meulbroek; & Sloan, R. (July 2001). Short-sellers, fundamental analysis, and stock returns. *Journal of Financial Economics.* Volume 61, Issue 1, pp. 77–106.
2. Alexander, C. (2008). *Market Risk Analysis, Pricing, Hedging and Trading Financial Instruments.* Hoboken NJ: John Wiley & Sons, p. 225.
3. Hagin, R. (2003). Investment Management. Hoboken NJ: John Wiley & Sons, p. 118.

7

Short Options and Levels of Risk

The installment strategy is designed to eliminate market risk in two situations: first, when a trader owns shares of stock and wants to eliminate market risk, and second, when a trader wants to freeze today's price per share for future purchase.

However, this requires execution of several short positions between entry of the strategy and expiration of the LEAPS long position. Exercise risk must be considered with each entry of a short position, and the timing of a close must also anticipate potential exercise risks and entry to a new, later-expiring position.

Unavoidable Risks

Exercise is the constant risk for any open short position. Upon opening a short option, you receive premium payment. However, at any time the short option moves in the money (stock price higher than a call's strike or lower than a put's strike), exercise risk becomes a reality.

At these times, traders may close a position for either a profit or loss, and then select a new short position with a different strike to avoid exercise risk. This may involve rolling forward to the same strike but a different expiration.

Risk itself extends beyond the options-specific risks. The entire concept of investing in the stock market often faces a larger risk, that of basic trust:

The decision to invest in stocks requires not only an assessment of the risk-return trade-off given the existing data, but also an act of faith (trust) that the data in our possession are reliable and that the overall system is fair.[1]

Trust goes to the fundamentals. Can an options trader intent on opening short positions within an installment strategy rely on fundamental analysis to select appropriate stocks? This question must be addressed so that the trader is reasonably certain that stock selection itself has been made based on reliable data. Only once that has been achieved can the trader move forward with confidence and consider the risks of exercise for the short option.

Risk Hedge Exercise

Exercise risk must be considered within the context of the installment strategy. If you own shares and enter a risk hedge (buying a LEAPS put and selling a series of short options over time), exercise of a current short option contains one of two consequences. Because you own shares, a short call is covered, and exercise leads to shares being called away. If the strike of the call is higher than your original purchase price per share, exercise sets up a capital gain. (If the strike is lower than your original cost per share, the result is a capital loss, mitigated by premium received for the call. For example, if your original price per share was $46 and you sold a 45-strike covered call for 2 ($200), the 1-point capital loss is offset by the 2-point profit in the covered call.)

Because exercise of a covered call does not create a net loss, it is not an alarming possibility. You can repurchase shares at a higher price if desired, leaving the LEAPS put intact at a lower strike. Or you can continue the strategy without repurchase, with the plan of paying for the LEAPS put while leaving it in place. In the event of a decline in the underlying price, the LEAPS put can eventually be sold for a net profit, assuming the ongoing series of short options reduces its basis to zero.

Another strategy is to wait and see how the underlying behaves. If price declines to the level of the original purchase price, you can repurchase shares and continue with the risk hedge. In this outcome, the net result is profit on both stock and option, without interfering with the long-term plans for continued ownership of stock and elimination of market risk.

Exercise of a short put poses a different outcome. In this case, you are required to accept another 100 shares of stock at the strike. Now, with a total of 200 shares of stock in your portfolio, the basis is the average of the two prices paid per share. In this situation, you face two choices. You can sell the additional shares and accept a loss (the loss is incurred because the purchase price was at the strike and higher than current market value). Or, you can keep the shares and double up on the risk hedge. This requires two actions. First, you purchase an additional LEAPS put so that the hedge covers all 200 shares; the selection of the strike may be different than the strike for the original 100 shares, based on current market value. The expiration may also be different. Second, with 200 shares in your portfolio, you now continue the risk hedge by selling two options each period rather than one. These may be covered calls, uncovered puts or a combination of the two.

Yet another alternative upon accepting exercise of a short put is to modify the risk hedge and convert it to a combined installment. By purchasing a LEAPS call in addition to the existing LEAPS put, you create either a straddle (with the same strike) or a spread (with a different strike). If expiration is the same, it is a vertical strategy, and if expiration is different, it creates either a horizontal spread or a diagonal spread. This "double hedge" is appealing because it creates a price hedge in both directions. If the underlying price advances, the call gains intrinsic value (and the LEAPS put is paid for by the series of short options). If the underlying price declines, the put gains intrinsic value (and the LEAPS call is paid for by the series of short options). Assuming the sale of options over time is adequate to cover either side, a move in the stock price will create profits in the other direction's LEAPS position.

Contingent Purchase Exercise

If you have opened a contingent purchase strategy, you probably do not own shares. The purpose of the strategy is to freeze a future purchase price at the strike. In this case, exercise results in one of several outcomes. For most traders in this situation, exercise is undesirable and should be avoided. However, depending on whether a call or a put is exercised, follow-up response will also be different.

If you open a short call and it is exercised, you are required to deliver 100 shares at the strike. However, because you do not own 100 shares, this requires two steps. You must purchase 100 shares at current market value and then use them to satisfy the call's exercise. If the difference between market value and strike is 3 points, this creates a loss of $300. If the difference is 12 points, your loss is $1200. Because the loss could be substantial, avoiding exercise of an uncovered call is a wise idea. To avoid exercise, always open out-of-the-money (OTM) strike calls, and plan to immediately close if the call moves close to the money, even if that means taking a loss. These can be rolled forward as well, preferably to a higher strike.

Because exercise of an uncovered call is a significant risk, it could make sense to focus primarily on uncovered puts, whose exercise would result in your receiving 100 shares. The loss in this case is a paper loss and acquiring shares might not be a negative result. The subsequent action could involve expanding the contingent strategy to add a put and set up a risk hedge while maintaining the contingent purchase call for future purchase of more shares. This is another version of action to set up a double hedge (contingent purchase for future share acquisition, and risk hedge to protect the position acquired through exercise of the put).

The growth rate of the options market has been accompanied by the observation that risks (such as exercise of an uncovered call) are not well understood in the market. Risk, as a "return characteristic" of the market, may be addressed with improved knowledge of the overall risk universe. With the growth in the market,

> has come controversy over the purpose served by options in the capital markets … the principal function of options is to provide a significant expansion of the patterns of portfolio returns available to investors. Such expansions make investors better off and add to the liquidity and efficiency of the capital markets.
>
> For investors to benefit from the additional investment opportunities provided by options, they must be informed as to the return characteristics of various option strategies.[2]

The importance of becoming an *informed* investor regarding return characteristics cannot be emphasized too much. For example, the uncovered call is the highest risk portion of any installment strategy, but this is easily overlooked in the desire to accomplish the goal of paying for a LEAPS position.

The selection of a short position as part of the contingent purchase contains greater risk when uncovered calls are part of the strategy. The uncovered call has greater risks than the covered call, because the gap at the time of exercise between strike and current market value could be large. At the same time being able to use both calls and puts is advantageous. In the ideal timing of one side or the other, you would open short puts at the bottom of a price swing, and close as price moves toward the center, and you would open short calls at the top of the price swing. In this manner, you can exploit both sides of the price movement, which reduces exercise risk.

The moneyness of the option matters greater as part of exercise avoidance. You will want to select options on both sides that are OTM, preferably with a buffer of several points. In this way, while exploiting time decay for short-term expiration terms, you also can escape exercise if the option begins moving unfavorably toward the money.

This is affected further by volatility in the underlying. The best time to open short positions is when volatility is high, because option premium is rich at those moments. However, after entering a short position, a reduction in volatility makes the position more likely to lose value rapidly (which is desirable because an opening sale can then be closed with a lower priced purchase to close). However, timing volatility is never easy, so this requires identification of strong reversal signals and confirmation at the point of entry.

For example, at a price peak, you may open an uncovered call at a strike with a buffer of several points above current price. In addition, you identify a reversal in a series of running gaps, a candlestick signal, momentum oscillator or volume spike, and find a separate confirmation signal also indicating reversal.

How much of a buffer do you need at these times? The more points you require in a buffer, the lower the premium. This leads traders to accept a lower buffer in exchange for a higher premium. However, the buffer may be quite small in one specific situation: when price has moved so strongly that it exceeds three standard deviations above the upper Bollinger Band.

The default of Bollinger Bands is two standard deviations, and price rarely remains outside of that zone for very long. When price moves out beyond three standard deviations, it never stays there for long. This is the ideal timing for opening a short position, using an uncovered call above the upper band or an uncovered put below the lower band.

For example, Fig. 7.1 shows an example of price moving above the three standard deviation upper Bollinger Band. This is extremely rare and will not be found on most charts. Price closed above on only one session, and then retreated immediately back into the range below the bank for the following week. However, price then gapped lower and continued declining.

Fig. 7.1 Price above three standard deviation upper Bollinger Band

The timing for an entry of an uncovered call would have been perfect on that single session when price moved above the three standard deviations. It is an extreme move, and at that point a close to the money call would have been priced attractively. The four sessions leading up to the move above the upper band were very rapid and contained gaps, so entry of a short call at this point would be well timed.

Covered Calls for Risk Reduction

The covered call is among the safest of options strategies, but it also contains risks. If the underlying declines below net basis (cost of stock minus option premium), the result is a paper loss. If the underlying rises far above the call's strike, the call will be exercised unless it is closed or rolled:

> It appears that covered call options give the investor the best of both worlds: a hedge against losses if stock price decline, and a higher return on equity if stock prices rise. Yet these benefits are not obtained without some cost: the investor's potential for profit is limited. Once the option is sold, the maximum obtainable profit is set, provided the investor holds both the stock and written option until expiration.[3]

Call writers must be willing to live with these risks. The maximum profit from writing covered calls is limited to the premium received; however, this is acceptable considering that the alternative is a buy-and-hold strategy, hoping for an exceptional capital gain. That can occur, but the covered call yields repetitive and consistent income. Accordingly, as part of the risk hedge strategy, it is the safest short-side strategy.

The worst-case outcome is exercise. In the event of exercise, shares are called away at a profit (assuming you picked a strike above your basis in stock). You increase that profit by the premium for the covered call.

Very short-term expiration is most desirable, because the strategy is set up to exploit time decay. Opening a covered call expiring in seven to ten days is ideal, because this is the period in which time decay is most accelerated. Selecting an OTM strike increases chances for success; even if the call moves in the money, chances are good that time decay will outpace intrinsic value, so that the position can be closed at a profit.

The covered call can be expanded to produce higher income. A ratio write occurs when you write more calls than you can cover. For example, if you own 300 shares and write four calls, it sets up a 4:3 ratio write. You can look at this as 75 percent coverage, or as a combination of three covered calls and one uncovered call. For example, as of May 14, 2018, IBM closed at $144.30 per share. If you purchased 300 shares of stock at $144.30 per share, and at the same time sold four calls at the 145 strike, you create a ratio write. Those calls were bid at 1.07 each, so four calls would have yielded $428, less estimated trading fees of $8, for a net of $420.

Risk levels are completely changed between covered calls and ratio writes, and this should not be ignored. The ratio write

> involves writing a number of naked call options as well as a number of covered options. The resulting position has both downside risk, as does a covered call, and unlimited upside risk, as does a naked write. The ratio write generally will provide much larger profits than either covered writing or naked writing if the underlying stock remains relatively unchanged during the life of the calls. However, the ratio write has two-sided risk, a quality absent from either covered or naked writing.[4]

With this risk profile in mind, a ratio write should follow the same guidelines as the 1:1 covered call: short expiration, OTM strike and proximity timed with the trading range swing. This means covered calls and ratio writes should be opened near the top of the swing (close to resistance), with the expectation that price will reverse and move down.

Because the ratio write is higher risk than the covered call, proximity to the upper Bollinger Band continues to set up the best possible timing. When price moves above the upper band, timing for a ratio write is ideal. If you find the unusual situation where price has moved above the three standard deviation band, the timing is improved even more.

Another variation on the covered call is the variable ratio write. In this version, two strikes are employed rather than one. For example, the IBM purchase of 300 shares may be accompanied by opening four short calls, two at the strike of 145 and two at the strike of 146. The 145 calls were bid at 1.07, so the total would have been $214 less estimated $6 trading fee, net $208. The 146 calls were bid at 0.70, so the two short calls would have yielded $140, minus $6 trading fee, net $134. The two positions together yielded $348.

This is $72 less than the one-strike ratio write, but the position offers considerably lower risks. If the calls move in the money in this situation, any of the short calls can be closed or rolled without needing to close out or roll the entire position. In this way, the variable ratio write can be converted to a 1:1 covered call by buying to close only one of the four open options.

In the risk hedge, when you own shares of the underlying and enter a position with covered calls or a ratio write, the purpose is to produce income to reduce the cost of a long-term LEAPS put, while also minimizing risk exposure. Considering the low risk of covered calls, they make the best vehicle for this purpose. If you are willing to assume higher risks to yield greater profits, the ratio write and variable ratio write are worth considering as well.

Uncovered Puts for the Same Risk Profile

The covered call offers limited risk exposure. The uncovered put has the same market risk and may also be used as a low-risk method to pay for a long-term option. This argument applies both to the risk hedge with a LEAPS put and a contingent purchase strategy with a LEAPS call. However, in the contingent purchase, the assumption is that you own no shares and want to freeze a future purchase at the strike of the call. The call would not be covered, so the uncovered put is a lower risk alternative.

Just as the short call should be opened near the top of the trading range, the short put should be opened near the bottom. This is the point where reversal is most likely, and if that occurs the short put will lose premium value and can be bought to close at a profit. The argument based on proximity of price to lower Bollinger Band applies with equal strength to that of the short call to upper Bollinger Band. It is the most advantageous position to open the short position.

The short put can move in the money when the underlying price declines. Therefore, slightly OTM strikes with short expiration are most desirable. There is a good chance in these conditions that rapidly declining time value will offset and even surpass increases in intrinsic value. As a result, the short put can be closed, perhaps at a small profit, or rolled forward to avoid exercise.

A variation on the short put is to apply the ratio concept usually applied to covered calls. In the case of the covered call, a ratio write is rationalized by the fact that it provides partial coverage. In the case of a short put, there is no coverage available, but the same principle of risk management can be applied. This principle is that the uncovered put ratio can be closed or rolled to avoid exercise.

For example, in the case of IBM which closed at $144.30 on May 14, 2018, if you do not own shares but want to enter a contingent purchase plan, you open a long-term LEAPS call. This is paid for with a series of short options, either calls or puts. The danger of calls is that exercise risk is considerable. With short puts, the risk is identical to covered call risks, so the application of a ratio makes sense to increase income in exchange for a small increase in risk. At that time, the 144 put (slightly below current price of $144.30) was bid at 1.14. If your intention was to buy 300 shares in the future, you would have opened three long LEAPS calls. To now offset that cost, you could sell three OTM puts. The 1:1 position would involve selling three 144 puts at a bid of 1.14, or $342 minus approximately $7, or $335 net.

A *ratio* version would involve selling four puts for a total of $456, minus $8, net $448. And a *variable ratio* of puts would combine two 144 puts for $228, minus $6, net $222; and two 143 puts at bid of 0.77, total $154, minus $6, net $148. The variable put ratio yields a total of $370. This is $78 below the ratio write but is considerable less risky.

Uncovered Calls and Varying Risk Levels

The uncovered call also plays a role in the installment purchase strategy. In the risk hedge, the assumption is that you own shares and use covered calls. However, the contingent purchase does not include covered calls; the uncovered put and the uncovered call can be used in combination.

The observation that the short call cannot be covered without ownership of stock is not entirely accurate. The ownership of a long-term LEAPS call does offset the sale of a call. In other words, if a short-term call is exercised, the long-term LEAPS call can be sold to satisfy the exercise. This means that a form of coverage does exist; the long call offsets the risk of the short call. However, it is not practical to assume that the long call will be used in this way. Because it is long term, the time value is extremely high. Selling that call to pay for an exercised short call will not be likely to end up as a net profit. The sale of the LEAPS call is likely to occur at a *lower* strike than the current value of stock. The intention of the installment strategy is to freeze today's price at that strike, so selling it to satisfy an exercised call is contrary to the purpose in entering the strategy.

A better alternative probably will be to pay the difference between current price and the exercised strike, take the loss and move forward with the strategy. The net loss increases the level of income required to pay for the LEAPS call, but this alternative is preferable. Because the underlying price will have risen in this situation, it translates to a favorable price movement in the underlying.

However, considering the risks of writing uncovered calls in any situation, when operating the contingent purchase strategy, uncovered puts are preferable. The exception is the ideal proximity and signal moment. An uncovered call is justified when four conditions are found:

1. Current price has advanced through upper Bollinger Band, especially if the price is higher than a three standard deviation version of the band.
2. A reversal signal is identified.
3. A strong confirmation signal is also found. Among the strongest of these are the volume spike, strong candlestick bearish reversal signals or Western technical signals such as double tops or island reversals.
4. The movement of the stock price to this position occurred quickly, in a series of sessions with gaps. This is the condition in which reversal is most likely.

Picking Calls or Puts Based on Price Proximity

The concept of price *proximity* is essential in successfully timing both entry and exit of short trades. The observation of price at the point of resistance or support identifies the likely point of reversal.

Equally important is moneyness of the option, or the distance from current price to strike. In selling an option, a prudent method is to build a buffer zone between price and OTM strike. However, for lower priced stocks, this is not always possible.

For example, as of the close of May 15, 2018, a comparison between three companies and their OTM call and put bids demonstrates the differences of return on both calls and puts, and the varying ability to set up buffer zones (Table 7.1).

The dollar values of bid prices for higher price issues are higher than for lower priced stocks, as you would expect. However, more important is the yield represented by each of the bid prices. The comparison is made between the bid quote and the current price per share. The buffer zones to the strikes farthest away from the money are using the 16-day expirations (Table 7.2).

This chart shows that higher priced stocks will tend to yield better returns on the current price, than lower priced stocks. Chipotle's call was 8.44 points OTM, and its 16-day call yielded 1.0 percent. Fedex's call was 7.66 points OTM, and its 16-day call yielded 0.5 percent, one-half the yield of Chipotle. And eBay's call was 1.92 points OTM, and its 16-day call yielded 0.2 percent.

The conclusion of this analysis is that setting up a buffer zone will be practical for higher priced stocks than for lower priced stocks. Does this mean the focus of an installment strategy should be on higher priced stocks? That is not necessarily the conclusion worth reaching. Rather, picking strong fundamental companies should be the first step, and selection of short positions reflects varying returns, as shown above. However, for lower strikes, the demand for earnings on a series of short options is also lower; a smaller net yield may be acceptable given the lower demand for dollar and percentage yield.

The proximity concern has two parts. The first part is timing of an entry based on proximity between price and trading range borders. The optimal timing for entry of a short call is when underlying price is close to resistance, or when it has moved through that price level. The optimal timing for entry of a short put is when underlying price is close to support, or when it has moved through that price level. However, entry at these points requires identification of a reversal signal and confirmation. Proximity points to the best price point, but the reversal signal is equally important.

Table 7.1 OTM options comparison

Strike	4-day Calls	4-day Puts	16-day Calls	16-day Puts
Chipotle (CMG) $426.56				
435	4.20		5.90	
432.50	5.00		6.90	
430	6.20		8.00	
427.50	7.39		9.10	
425		6.80		8.70
422.50		5.70		7.40
420		4.80		6.50
417.50		4.10		5.70
Fedex Corp. (FDX) $247.34				
255	0.70		1.26	
252.50	1.23		1.92	
250	1.96		2.84	
247.50	3.20		4.05	
245		2.16		2.86
242.50		1.44		2.08
240		0.96		1.49
237.50		0.64		1.02
eBay Corp. (EBAY) $38.08				
40	0.04		0.08	
39.50	0.09		0.14	
39	0.18		0.29	
38.50	0.34		0.47	
38		0.47		0.59
37.50		0.28		0.40
37		0.17		0.26
36.50		0.10		0.17

Table 7.2 Company comparison

Company	Price	Strike	Premium	%
Chipotle	$426.56	435 (call)	5.90	1.0
		417.50 (put)	5.70	1.3
Fedex	$247.34	255 (call)	1.26	0.5
		237.50 (put)	1.02	0.4
eBay	$38.08	40 (call)	0.08	0.2
		36.50 (put)	0.17	0.4

The second proximity issue is the buffer zone between current price of the underlying and strike of the short call or put. In the example, the highest priced stock (Chipotle) provided an 8.44-point buffer zone on the call side, and premium of 5.90. Adding the point spread to the premium, the total short call buffer was 14.34 points (8.44 + 5.90). The lowest priced put provided a buffer zone of 9.06 points between price and strike, and the put yielded 5.70. The total buffer in this case was 14.76 points (9.06 + 5.70).

Although this buffer zone is more attractive than the comparable zone for lower priced stocks, that is not the entire story. eBay provided buffer zones of 1.92 points (call) and 1.58 points (put). Adding the very small premium, the adjusted zones were 1.96 points (short call) and 1.75 points (short put). However, eBay's price of 38.08 was approximately 9 percent of the price of Chipotle. Adjusting premium levels and price spreads based on differences in the underlying price makes the proximity more comparable. If you purchased 1100 shares of eBay and paid $38.08 per share, the value would be close to the value of 100 shares of Chipotle. However, the relative value of 11 short calls or puts on 1100 shares of eBay versus 100 shares of Chipotle would not be equal. The percentage yields on the identified OTM calls and puts tell the story. The conclusion is that even when the approximate equity value is equalizer between two or more different underlyings, the percentage yield remains fixed.

The higher priced stocks yield not only larger dollar value premium, but more attractive yields as well. However, this will not always be the case. To ensure that you select the most favorable underlyings, strikes and proximity, make complete and detailed comparisons.

Exploiting Time Decay

Timing entry and exit requires observation of time decay and when it is maximized. For short positions, opening trades set to expire in one to two weeks in the desired time range to exploit rapidly declining time value.

Two dates are of greatest interest in this timing of trade entry and exit. First is the Friday before expiration. There are seven days remaining until the last trading day, but only five trading days. As a result, between Friday and Monday, the typical option loses 33 percent of remaining time value; a $100 premium will decline by Monday's open to $66. However, because off-hours activity over three days can create unexpected movement in the underlying, there is always a risk associated with holding a short position open over a weekend.

The second key date is Thursday, the day before last trading day. On average, options will lose 32 percent of remaining time value between Thursday's close and Friday's open.

Timing entry for Friday and the following Thursday in expiration week improves chances for a successful short option trade. The position can then be bought to close on Monday and again on the last trading day, the following Friday.[5]

What can you do when the underlying price moves against you? If your short option ends up in the money right before expiration, if you take no action it will be exercised. In some situations, this is an acceptable outcome. However, assuming your purpose in opening a risk hedge or installment purchase is to provide control over a future price of shares, exercise normally would be avoided. This is accomplished by closing the position (at a profit or at a loss) or rolling forward to a later expiration.

In rolling forward, if you can break even on the net credit and debit and replace the current strike with a higher one (for short calls) or a lower one (for short puts), that is a good justification for the forward roll. However, going to the next expiration will normally require that you use the same strike unless you are willing to pay a net debit. A problem in rolling forward beyond the next strike is that this leaves your position exposed for a longer period. Compare the risk of tying up capital for longer than you want, versus the net loss suffered by closing the position. Rolling forward helps manage risk, but it is not always as advisable as closing and taking a small loss.

The forms of risk short sellers face can take many forms. Selling calls and puts is one form of trade that comes with risks, and when the price direction moves against your short position, you could end up with larger losses than you can afford. The solution to this is to keep expiration terms short, build in a buffer zone, time entry and exit based on proximity and strong reversal signals and exit a position when it begins moving against you (underlying trending up against a short call or trending down against a short put).

Another way to mitigate the risks you face with installment strategies is to consider alternatives to short positions. These alternatives include an array of spreads, straddles and synthetic positions.

Notes

1. Guiso, L., Sapienza, P., & Zingales, L. (2008). Trusting the stock market. *The Journal of Finance*, Volume 63, No. 6, pp. 2557–2600.
2. Merton, R., Scholes, M., & Gladstein, M. (1978). The returns and risk of alternative call option portfolio investment strategies. *The Journal of Business*, Volume 51, No. 2, pp. 183–242.
3. Mueller, P. (1981). Covered options: An alternative investment strategy. *Financial Management*, Volume 10, No. 4, pp. 64–71.
4. McMillan, L. (2002). *Options as a Strategic Investment*, 4th Ed. New York: New York Institute of Finance, p. 146.
5. Augen, J. (2009). *Trading Options at Expiration*. Upper Saddle River NJ: FT Press, p. 41.

8

Alternative Offsets Beyond Short Calls or Short Puts

Installment strategies are by no means limited to the single-option contingent purchase or risk hedge. Both varieties can be expanded to incorporate numerous combinations in the form of spreads, straddles and ratios created synthetically.

A trader can adjust not only potential profit levels by selection of advanced strategies but also to engineer lower (or higher) levels of risk. This means that the use of installment positions can involve any number of options positions and swing trading techniques.

Synthetic Stock

The first adjustment in the installment strategy is the use of synthetic stock positions. There are two of these: synthetic long stock and synthetic short stock. This is the creation of a separate trade investment designed to provide leverage as well as profit:

> In the sense that a synthetic is a new net position created as the result of two or more real positions in a market … [it] is not aimed at hedging, however, but at creating a new and financially positive investment or borrowing situation.[1]

These newly created instruments are referred to as "synthetic" positions because, although only options are involved, they duplicate price movement in the underlying stock, moving point for point in either direction. As the titles indicate, a synthetic long stock performs best when the underlying stock advances in price, and the synthetic short stock favors a decline in the underlying.

Although synthetics often are compared to ownership of stock as identical, this is not quite true. A synthetic long stock position involves a long call, which enables the trader to control 100 shares. However, "the option strategist does not collect dividends, whereas the stock owner does."[2]

This does not apply in cases when the underlying does not pay a dividend; in that case, the synthetic long stock is a substitute for stock ownership at a much lower cost. It combines a long call and a short put, with the same strike and the same expiration. The net debit or credit for this position will be very small and depends on whether the bid/ask spread is wide or narrow, and on whether the ask price of the call is higher or lower than the bid price of the put.

For example, Target (TGT) closed on May 18, 2018, at $75.94 per share. A synthetic long stock position can be opened at the 76 strike (only 6 cents higher than the price per share of the underlying), using the following:

Buy 76 call, ask 2.21, plus trading fees = $226
Sell 76 put, bid 2.09, less trading fees = $204
Net debit = $22

In this example, as price moves, so does the net value of the options. Table 8.1 summarizes price activity at a variety of prices as of expiration.

At each price point, the net difference between the underlying profit or loss and the synthetic position profit or loss is $28. This is the net of the debit for the synthetic long stock plus the net difference between strike and underlying price at the time of entry:

Net debit $22
Strike minus underlying price 6
Total $28

Table 8.1 Target, synthetic long stock

Price of underlying ($)	Long call	Short put	Net options	Stock profit
82	+374	+204	+578	+606
80	+174	+204	+378	+406
78	−26	+204	+178	+206
76	−226	+204	−22	+06
74	−226	+4	−222	−194
72	−226	−196	−422	−394
70	−226	−396	−622	−594

The synthetic long stock gains value as the underlying price rises. The outcome is superior to only selling a put, which would yield $204 if the underlying rose to $82 per share, versus $578 profit in the synthetic long stock. The same position loses value, however, if the underlying price declines. If the stock value fell to $70 per share, the synthetic loses $622, versus only $226 for a short call or $396 for a short put. The synthetic long stock position is exceptional leverage at a debit of only $22, but the outcome relies on whether the underlying price rises or falls. For example, with Target (TGT) closing at $75.94 on May 18, 2018, the following positions could have been opened to set up a synthetic short stock position:

> Buy 76 put, ask 2.23, plus trading fees = $228
> Sell 76 call, bid 2.12, less trading fees = $207
> Net debit = $21

As price moves, so does the net value of the options. Table 8.2 summarizes price activity at a variety of prices as of expiration.

The synthetic short stock gains value as the underlying price falls. For example, with Target (TGT) closing at $75.94 on May 18, 2018, the following positions could have been opened to set up a synthetic short stock position:

> Buy 76 put, ask 2.23, plus trading fees = $228
> Sell 76 call, bid 2.12, less trading fees = $207
> Net debit = $21

At any price point as of expiration, the net difference between gain or loss in the underlying and gain or loss in the synthetic short stock is equal to $15, the net difference between the debit paid for the position and the distance from the stock price to the strike:

Table 8.2 Target, synthetic short stock

Price of underlying ($)	Long put	Short call	Net options	Stock profit
82	−228	−393	−621	+606
80	−228	−193	−421	+406
78	−228	+7	−221	+206
76	−228	+207	−21	+06
74	−28	+207	+179	−194
72	+172	+207	+379	−394
70	+372	+207	+579	−594

Net debit	$21
Strike minus underlying price	−6
Net difference	$15

The selection of a synthetic long or synthetic short position relies on whether you believe the stock price is likely to rise or fall. For a very small net cost, the synthetic could be set up with two strikes, and selection of both a long and a short position.

For example, a "box" version of the synthetic combining a long and a short could be set up with the following positions:

<u>Long</u>

Buy 76.50 call, ask 1.76, plus trading fees = $181

Sell 76.50 put, bid 2.20, less trading fees = $215

Net credit = $34

<u>Short</u>

Buy 75.50 put, ask 1.77, plus trading fees = $182

Sell 75.50 call, bid 2.21, less trading fees = $216

Net credit = $34

Combined net credit = $68

For a net credit of $68, the box synthetic stock could benefit or suffer with stock movement in either direction. This position demands considerable management to ensure that losses in either direction do not set up overall net losses.

The box synthetic could also be set up diagonally, which involves selecting different expiration dates for each of the two positions. However, this requires that the underlying progress in one direction by the first expiration, and then move in the opposite direction by the second expiration. This outcome would be ideal, but also is impossible to predict ahead of time. Considering the complexity of the synthetic box spread, staying with a single long or short makes more sense.

Timing depends on proximity of the underlying, just as it does in the selection of a single short call or short put. The synthetic long stock position is timed well when entered at or near the bottom of a price swing within the trading range. It is a relative low-risk strategy because the short put has the same market risk as the covered call. The synthetic short position is bearish and should be entered in proximity to resistance and in anticipation of a price swing to the downside. This is a higher risk strategy because it includes an uncovered call, which contains higher risk than the uncovered put.

However, even with the inherent higher risk of synthetic short stock, it remains far less risky than the alternatives: buying puts or shorting stock. Buying puts is profitable when underlying prices fall, but the breakeven is the strike of the put minus the cost of the put; the risk is that an underlying price will not decline enough below this breakeven point. Shorting stock is much higher risk because the potential loss could be substantial. In addition, shorting stock is a complex and potentially high-risk trade:

> Taking a short position in a stock is a more complex transaction than just clicking a mouse and entering a short sell order in XYZ. To short a stock, a trader must borrow the shares of XYZ from a trader or investor who holds a long position in XYZ. Due to a variety of circumstances, at times the ability to borrow shares of a stock when one wants to gain short exposure may not exist. A so-called "hard to borrow" stock may be costly to borrow in order to execute a short, so using options to create a synthetic short payoff is an excellent alternative.[3]

The synthetic short stock risk due to the short call can be mitigated. If a trader also owns 100 shares of the underlying, the call is covered, and the risk of an uncovered call is eliminated.

Vertical and Diagonal Spreads

The short side of an installment strategy can also be executed with a credit spread—a spread setting up receipt of cash, versus payment (a debit spread).

The credit spread generates income, but it is the net difference between a long and a short option. It will not bring in the level of cash as that of a single option, so the spread should be used in times when volatility is high and the direction of price movement in the underlying for the short term is uncertain. The benefit of a spread is that, while it limits income, it also limits possible net loss.

A vertical spread combines a long and a short call, or a long and a short put. The expiration date is the same for both sides in a vertical spread, and the degree of profit or loss is determined by the distance between the two strikes. A *bullish* vertical spread consists of puts, and a *bearish* credit spread consists of calls.

For example, Chipotle was trading at $435.51 at the close of May 23, 2018. The price had jumped 95 points in a single day on April 26 and was trading at the higher price level for the past month. This stock chart is shown in Fig. 8.1.

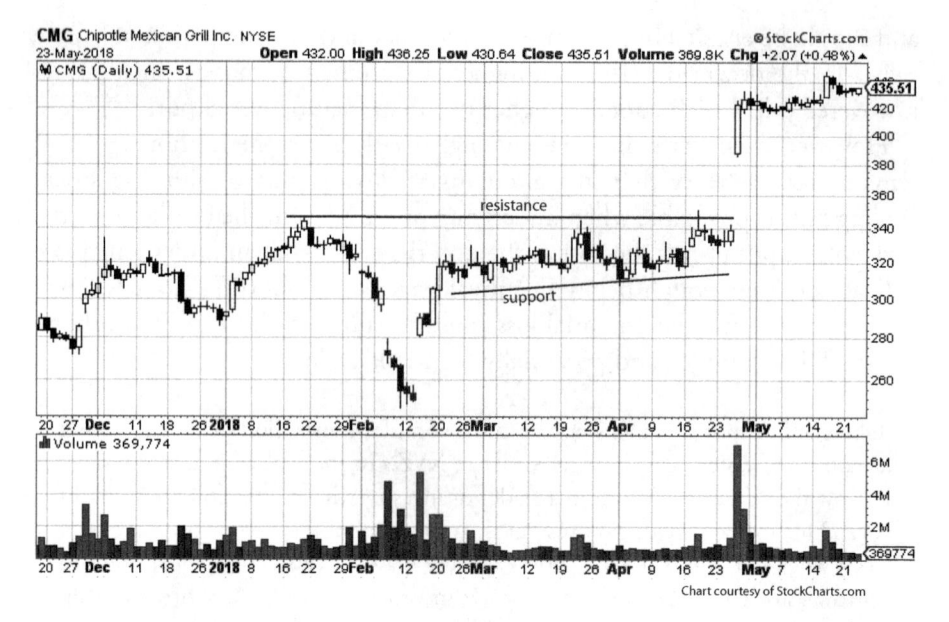

Fig. 8.1 Chipotle (CMG)

You have a long-term LEAPS on this company, but your dilemma now is that you do not know which direction the stock will move next. Will it retreat and fill the gap from the previous month? Or will the higher price level become a new trading range?

This is precisely the condition in which a credit spread will work. You generate a net credit, but you do not have the exposure you would have with a single short option. The 8-day and 29-day options in a range of five strikes are summarized in Table 8.3.

A bullish credit spread employs puts. Two examples:

8-day option

Buy one 432.50 put, ask 4.80, plus trading fee = $485
Sell one 440 put, bid 8.30, less trading fee = $825
    Net credit = $340

29-day option

Buy one 430 put, ask 11.90, plus trading fee = $1195
Sell one 437.50 put, bid 13.00, less trading fee = $1295
    Net credit = $100

Table 8.3 Option listings, Chipotle (CMG)

	Calls		Puts	
	Bid	Ask	Bid	Ask
June 1 Strike				
430	9.20	9.70	3.50	3.90
432.50	7.60	8.20	4.40	4.80
435	6.20	6.70	5.50	6.00
437.50	5.20	5.50	6.80	7.30
440	4.20	4.50	8.30	8.80
June 22 Strike				
430	15.80	16.90	9.40	11.90
432.50	14.40	15.60	10.60	11.70
435	13.00	14.10	11.60	12.20
437.50	11.80	13.40	13.00	16.50
440	10.60	12.60	14.30	17.40

Source: Charles Schwab & Co.
Options listings 5/23/18
CMG $435.51 (May 23, 2018)

The 29-day options are more expensive, but the net credit is less than for the 8-day options. Using the shorter term for a vertical credit spread, the example yields $340 net. In comparison, selling an out-of-the-money (OTM) call at a 440 strike as a single-option trade yields $415 (4.20 strike less trading fee). For $75 less, the vertical put spread offers maximum risk of $750 (the difference between the strikes), which is a limited risk. The single call could have much greater risk if the stock price rises above the 440 strike.

The same rationale applies to a bearish credit spread, which is based on calls. An example can be based on the same options listings, and the following are examples of two bearish credit spreads:

> 8-day option
>
> Buy one 440 call, ask 4.50, plus trading fee = $455
>
> Sell one 430 call, bid 9.20, less trading fee = $915
>
> Net credit = $460
>
> 29-day option
>
> Buy one 440 call, ask 12.60, plus trading fee = $1265
>
> Sell one 430 call, bid 15.80, less trading fee = $1575
>
> Net credit = $310

This example is like the bullish one. The shorter term options offer a more attractive spread, with a net credit of $460 versus the longer term spread of only $310. Opening a credit spread for eight days and gaining a credit of $460 compares to selling a single OTM put with a 432.50 strike, which is valued at 4.40; this yields a net of $435 after subtracting trading fees. In this example, the credit spread has maximum risk of 10 points, of $1000. However, selling a single put could be significantly higher risk. Recalling that the price jumped 95 points in a single day the month before, the exercise risk is considerable.

The spread can also be set up as a diagonal. For example, a bullish diagonal spread using puts could combine the sale of a 435 put and the purchase of a later expiring 430 put. Based on the two expiration cycles previously introduced, this would set up the following:

<u>8-day option</u>

Sell one 435 put, bid 5.50, less trading fee = $545

<u>29-day option</u>

Buy one 430 put, ask 11.90, plus trading fee = $1195

Net debit = $650

Although this produces a net debit, it can be adjusted. Once the eight-day put expires, it can be replaced with a weekly option to reduce the net cost. Between the two strikes used in the example, there are two additional expiration cycles (based on the current timing, these would be 15-day and 22-day, although by the time these were employed, each would be 7-day or 8-day expirations).

By replacing one short-term short position with another, either once or twice, the net debit could be reduced, perhaps even converted to a net credit. The installment method in this example refers not only to the comparison between a LEAPS position and current net credits, but also to the diagonal spread.

The diagonal can also be reversed, buying a shorter term and selling a longer term put to set up a net credit. However, this is not the optimal use of the diagonal spread. Its purpose is to set up more rapid time decay for a short position expiring sooner, versus slower time decay for a long put expiring later.

The same diagonal strategy can be used in anticipation of a bearish move, using calls to set up the position. In that case, the shorter term call should be an OTM strike, and the longer term call an in-the-money (ITM) strike or lower OTM strike. The selection of the strikes determines the net credit (or in a diagonal, the net debit), which also defines maximum risk. In both vertical and diagonal spreads, maximum risk is equal to the difference between strikes, minus a net credit or plus a net debit.

The vertical and diagonal spread are defensive alternatives to single-option short positions, to be used when you are unsure about the direction of the underlying in short-term price movement.

Straddles and Strangles

The vertical and diagonal spread expand the possibilities for offsetting a LEAPS cost, but both profits and losses are limited. Another approach is to use straddles or strangles to achieve the desired short payment, and with both strategies opened as short positions, it is possible to double the credits and accelerate the income level.

A *covered straddle* combines two positions: a covered call and an uncovered put. The strikes and expiration are identical. Because the uncovered put's market risk is the same as the market risk of the covered call, the covered straddle is a reasonably low-cost strategy. It should be used for low-volatility underlying conditions, however. The most desirable outcome is for very little movement, hoping for both sides to expire worthless or lose enough time value to be closed at a profit. Expiration should be very short term for the covered straddle, the same rule applied to all short positions. This exploits rapid time decay.

For example, a company with a three-month consolidation trend is FedEx. It traded between $233 and $255 and at the point of the chart, the price was close to the top of its range. Opening a covered straddle at this point would be one way to generate a credit. The chart for FedEx is shown in Fig. 8.2.

Options available at the closing price of $250.47 are shown in Table 8.4.

Opening a covered straddle with 8-day options or 15-day options, using at the money (ATM), combines the following possibilities:

> 8-day option
>
> Sell one 250 call, bid 2.87, less trading fee = $282
>
> Sell one 250 put, bid 2.16, less trading fee = $211
>
>   Total credit = $493

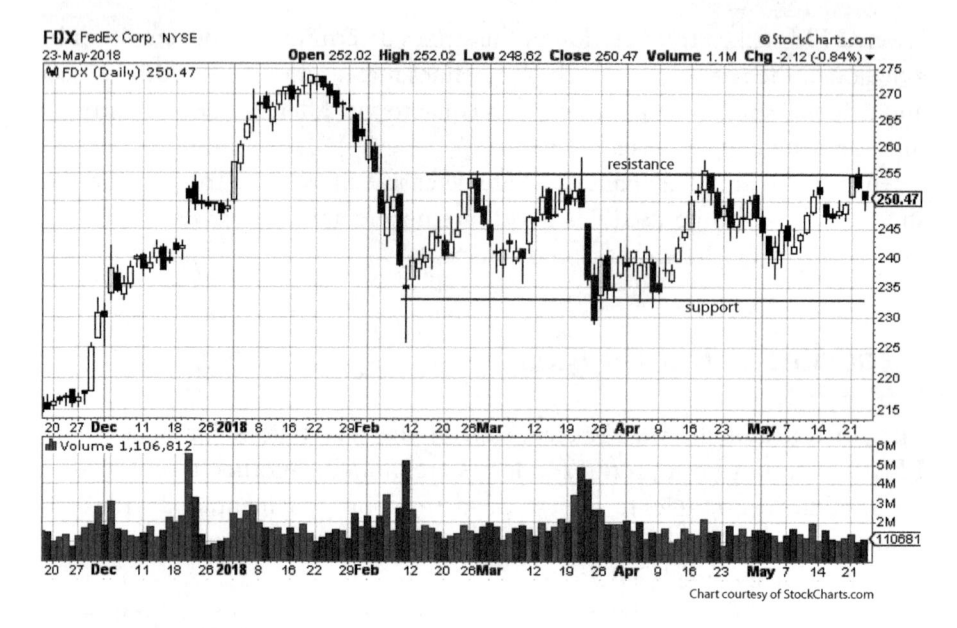

Fig. 8.2 Covered straddle

Table 8.4 Options listings, FedEx (FDX)

	Calls		Puts	
	Bid	Ask	Bid	Ask
June 1 Strike				
245	6.30	6.75	0.78	0.89
250	2.87	3.10	2.16	2.44
255	0.91	1.00	5.10	5.40
June 8 Strike				
245	6.75	7.60	1.51	1.60
250	3.95	4.05	3.10	3.25
255	1.68	1.89	5.80	6.15

Source: Charles Schwab & Co.
Options listings 5/23/18
FDX $250.47 (May 23, 2018)

<u>15-day option</u>

Sell one 250 call, bid 3.95, less trading fee = $390

Sell one 250 put, bid 3.10, less trading fee = $305

Total credit = $695

Selecting the longer term options yields more than $200 more income. However, it will not be as profitable over the long term as working with the shorter term options. Time decay will be rapid for these, but for the 15-day options, not as much time decay will occur until the following week. By opening a series of seven-day to ten-day positions week after week, the most advantageous outcomes are likely. Credits in the range of the high $400s week after week are more desirable than a two-week average of the high $600s.

Besides the higher income from shorter term options, risk is lower for short term as well. The longer short positions are left open, the more the impact of underlying price movement. For the eight-day options, even if the short call or put move in the money, it may be possible to close at a profit. Time decay may outpace intrinsic value when expiration is close.

A variation on the covered straddle is the *covered strangle*. This position is used when you own 100 shares, just like the covered straddle. The difference is that in the strangle, strikes are adjusted so that both are OTM. This yields lower credits, but also reduces market risks. The FedEx example could be converted to a covered strangle with the following positions:

8-day option

Sell one 255 call, bid 0.91, less trading fee = $86
Sell one 245 put, bid 0.78, less trading fee = $73
    Total credit = $159

15-day option

Sell one 255 call, bid 1.68, less trading fee = $163
Sell one 245 put, bid 1.51, less trading fee = $146
    Total credit = $309

Because both sides are OTM rather than ATM, total income is significantly lower than for the straddle. The same rationale concerning selection of expiration applies. The shorter term options are more desirable because time decay will be rapid.

In this example, a buffer zone of 5 points in either direction protects against exercise unless the underlying moves one of the short options in the money. With rapid time decay for the eight-day options, the modest income of $159 is relatively safe when compared to the ATM straddle.

The straddle and the strangle can also be opened without coverage. This increases risk because the call side is uncovered. The timing of an uncovered straddle or strangle should be coordinated with the price pattern. The chart for FedEx showed that price was close to the top of its three-month consolidation range, so the timing of an uncovered straddle or strangle was correct. In a more volatile underlying, the uncovered straddle or strangle is a higher risk method for paying down the cost of the LEAPS option.

Iron Butterfly

The spread and straddle can be useful alternatives to one-option short positions. A further expansion of the spread is the butterfly, and the *iron butterfly* is one of the most promising of these strategies.

This is a strategy in a family of *wing spreads*, so called because they are names for flying creatures (e.g. butterflies and condors). The iron butterfly combines a bear call spread and a bull put spread (each producing a net credit). Each side is structured around the current price of the underlying, with positions above and below. In a non-iron butterfly, a net debit is the result, whereas the iron butterfly sets up as a net credit. Several outcomes are possible, including taking of profits due to time decay:

> Ideally the stock will remain between the lower and higher strikes, with the maximum profit occurring if the options expire when the stock is priced at the central strike price. In this ideal scenario, effectively all the options expire worthless, and you just keep the combined net credit.[4]

The iron butterfly sets up a short ATM put and a long OTM put, and a short ATM call and a long OTM call. For example, an iron butterfly could be opened on Tesla (TSLA) as of May 23. The current declining trading range revealed the distance between resistance and support was shrinking. However, in the recent past, moments of volatility had appeared, making the iron butterfly potentially a worthwhile alternative to opening single-contract short options. Tesla's chart is shown in Fig. 8.3.

As of the ending date of the chart, an iron butterfly could be constructed from options expiring in either 8 days or 15 days, and this is summarized in Table 8.5.

An iron butterfly can be set up with either expiration date with the following positions:

Alternative Offsets Beyond Short Calls or Short Puts

Fig. 8.3 Iron butterfly

Table 8.5 Option listings, Tesla (TSLA)

	Calls		Puts	
	Bid	Ask	Bid	Ask
June 1 Strike				
275	9.05	9.35	5.05	5.25
280	6.25	6.45	7.20	7.50
285	4.10	4.30	9.95	10.35
June 8 Strike				
275	11.80	12.15	7.85	8.15
280	9.10	9.35	10.10	10.45
285	6.80	7.05	12.80	13.15

Source: Charles Schwab & Co.
Options listings 5/23/18
TSLA $279.07 (May 23, 2018)

<u>8-day option</u>

Buy one 275 put, ask 5.25, plus trading fee = −$530

Sell one 280 put, bid 7.20, less trading fee = $715

Sell one 280 call, bid 6.25, less trading fee = $620

Buy one 285 call, ask 4.30, plus trading fee = −$435

Net credit = $370

15-day option

Buy one 275 put, ask 8.15, plus trading fee = –$820
Sell one 280 put, bid 10.10, less trading fee = $1005
Sell one 280 call, bid 9.10, less trading fee = $905
Buy one 285 call, ask 7.05, plus trading fee = –$710
Net credit = $380

The outcomes for each of these positions are very close in net credit. The selection of one expiration over the other depends on whether the short-position time decay is of greater value than the offsetting long-position time decay. Because the net of all four options generates a credit, short-term time decay for the 8-day options is more desirable and will be likely to generate profits more rapidly than the 15-day options.

Closing the Long-Term Option at a Profit

The final alternative to continuing to sell short-term options (as single contracts or in one of the spread or straddle variations) is to close the LEAPS and take profits, ending the strategy early.

This enables you to take profits and to end the installment strategy as a success. However, this also contradicts the longer term goal of the installment. The contingent purchase is intended to freeze the future price for possible purpose, assuming the underlying advances above the strike. Because the cost of the LEAPS call will be taken down to zero, the contingent purchase strategy provides great flexibility. The risk hedge is used when you own shares and want to eliminate market risk below the strike, a hedge with zero cost (assuming it is held open and paid for with short options between entry and expiration).

As portfolio management strategies, both variations have long-term benefits. It does not always make sense to close the LEAPS, even when profits can be taken. From the point of view of a swing-trading strategy based on the use of options, closing when profits can be taken makes sense. However, the installment strategies are not swing trades, but portfolio management strategies. This means that early close of the LEAPS does not usually make sense.

Exceptions will be found, of course. These exceptions make it rational to close early and seek other methods for portfolio management, including the possibility of closing an equity position and replacing it with another. Among these exceptions are the following:

1. The Company's Fundamentals Have Changed The fundamentals can and do change over time. If the changes are negative, it makes sense to close out all options and to sell shares, and then seek an alternative with stronger fundamentals. Tests should include dividend yield and dividend per share, long-term debt to capitalization ratio, annual price/earnings (P/E) range, trends in revenue and earnings and trends in bet return.

2. Premium History of Short Options Has Been Disappointing In some instances, a lower than expected level of underlying volatility sets up conditions for lower than expected premium on short-term calls or puts. This could make it difficult to pay for the LEAPS position by expiration. Given that the LEAPS currently is profitable, closing out the installment positions makes sense. An examination of the fundamentals may also be justified, with the possibility of selling shares and buying shares of a stronger candidate.

3. Price Behavior of the Underlying Has Not Acted as Expected The installment strategy makes sense when price is volatile. Because volatility presents risk, installment option strategies are hedges. Expectation of bullish behavior makes sense for the contingent purchase. If you own shares and are concerned with market risk, the risk hedge makes sense. However, if the underlying price does not perform as expected at the time the strategy was entered, selling a profitable LEAPS makes sense, after which it also makes sense to look for an alternative company with more robust price volatility.

In opening an installment strategy, whether based on future purchase or risk hedge, there are many choices beyond selling single short calls or puts. It is also possible to expand the basic strategies. Beyond one LEAPS contract and one strategy or combination to offset its cost, you can expand the entire strategy to a more complex hedge that benefits you when prices rise or fall, and when the short side is also expanded to trade multiple contracts.

Notes

1. Greenleaf, R. (1989). Synthetic instruments. *Financial Analysts Journal*, Volume 45, No. 2, pp. 71–73.
2. McMillan, L. (2002). *Options as a Strategic Investment*, 4th Ed. New York: New York Institute of Finance, p. 323.
3. Rhoads, Russell (2011). *Option Spread Trading: A Comprehensive Guide to Strategies and Tactics*. Hoboken NJ: Wiley, p. 48.
4. Cohen, Guy. (2005). *The Bible of Options Strategies: The Definitive Guide for Practical Trading Strategies*. Upper Saddle River NJ: FT Press, 2005, p. 37.

9

Combining the Short Offset Alternatives

Current Price Proximity

The first step in reducing the initial risk of the long-term LEAPS is to observe proximity between strike to resistance or support, proximity of price to strike and, finally, proximity to reversal signals to the borders of the trading range.

The same observations of proximity apply with equal importance to the selection of strategies for short-term short calls or puts. These are designed to pay for the LEAPS cost over time, so that proximity ultimately determines whether positions are well timed or poorly timed for the overall strategic concerns.

In analyzing proximity for options strikes and stock price behavior, it is crucial to make distinctions between reality and myth. It has been observed that many "folk superstitions and many common assertions about stock market behavior rest upon similar reasoning, and often have the same degree of validity."[1]

To the serious trader, this means that reliance on proximity, by itself, is not adequate for timing of entry or exit in short options positions. You need to locate confirmation of reversal in addition to reversal, make note of the strength or weakness of proximity and use a set of signals collectively to improve overall trade timing.

Proximity of Strike to Resistance or Support

The first concern should be proximity of the selected strike to resistance or support. For the long-term long LEAPS, proximity depends on the type of option. In entering a contingent purchase strategy, the best position for opening the call is at the bottom of the price swing. For example, in Fig. 9.1, there are several key proximity points for entering a contingent purchase.

The chart opens at a price level of under $30 per share. Opening a LEAPS call with a 30 strike would be exceptionally well timed. However, with hindsight this is obvious; analysis of the previous six months shows that price had risen from $21 per share up to $28, so in the moment, the proximity advantage was not apparent.

A more easily observed proximity for entering a call was found in the first week of February, when price had declined from a high of $41 down to about $33. At this point in the first week of February, the long lower shadow of February 5 indicated weakness on the sell side and likely new establishment of support.

Another opportunity was presented in the last week of March and again in the last week of April. For timing entry for a LEAPS call, these positions of price presented the best proximity.

The chart also identified opportunities for entering a LEAPS put. If you owned shares and wanted to set up a risk hedge, proximity was excellent at $45 per share from mid-February to mid-March, and again, in late April and late May.

Fig. 9.1 Proximity of strike to resistance or support

Once a position is opened with a LEAPS, the same swing trading proximity points are observed for opening short-term short puts or calls to begin the process of paying for the long position. As price levels settled in April to a consolidation trend between $33 and $38 per share, two phenomena are observed. First, opportunities for volatility-based timing were reduced, but the timing risk was reduced as well. In this situation, short-term options will yield lower profits, but can be opened and closed with higher confidence that exercise risk is low.

Proximity of Price to Strike

The second proximity-based concern is between price and strike, or the moneyness of options selected, both for LEAPS selection and for short trades. This proximity—or better known as the "moneyness" of an option—is misunderstood by some traders as defining the profitability of an option. Moneyness only describes the distance between price and strike and does not define profit potential. Moneyness

> is *not* indicative of whether the trade is profitable. For example, an in-the-money option can be bought and then later sold for either a profit or a loss. So can out-of-the-money or at-the-money options, for that matter.[2]

The identification of moneyness proximity helps you to select the short trade. A desirable attribute of such a trade is accomplishing an acceptable premium *and* a buffer between price of the underlying and strike of the option. With this buffer, it is possible to escape a position moving in the wrong direction before the option goes in the money. The result: a loss will be small and, possibly, a modest profit can be realized.

At the time of entering either an installment purchase or a risk hedge strategy, considerations include the desired strike and its moneyness. If you are opening an installment purchase strategy, what price do you want to freeze for possible future purchase? For most situations, the price should be close to the current price per share. Opening a LEAPS call below that level will be expensive, and the farther below, the more expensive the call will be. If you are opening a risk hedge, meaning you own shares, one of two strikes will make sense. First is the price paid to acquire shares. In picking this strike, you intend to eliminate all market risk below your basis. Second is the current price, assuming it is higher than your basis. With this selection, if the stock price falls, you will be able to exercise the put and sell shares at a price higher than your basis.

Once the LEAPS has been opened, the proximity question is raised once again. For each short option you open, the concern must be exercise. This risk may be avoided by focusing on very short-term expiration terms, preferably one week or less. Time decay will be rapid during this period, so it is advantageous to open out-of-the-money (OTM) positions. However, a balance must be struck between the OTM distance from strike to price versus the bid price of the option. The more the strike is moved away from the current price, the less you will receive for selling the position. The closer to the money, the greater the premium, but the greater the exercise risk.

This is a dilemma. The balance between exercise risk and premium income is mitigated by planning to close at a profit as soon as adequate time decay has occurred. Staying very close to the money with short positions probably is the most advantageous selection, if you can track the position and to time a buy to close trade. In this case, taking a small profit is justified. Not only is that profit realized, but you are then free to sell to open a new, later expiring position with strike based on recent underlying price movement.

Setting up a bubble between price and OTM strike reduces exercise risk considerably, but it is not always possible to achieve and still generate adequate premium income to justify opening the position. This is more possible on higher priced stocks, where the dollar value of premium is higher. However, if those higher priced stocks also are more volatile, the exercise risk may become severe.

Does it ever make sense to open short in-the-money (ITM) positions? In the case of short calls opening when stock is also owned (as in a risk hedge), an ITM position after stock appreciation may set up the prospect of combining an attractive option premium with a capital gain in stock. This brings the risk hedge to a conclusion. However, because stock will have appreciated in value, the original hedge against a price decline did not materialize.

After exercise of a short call and having stock called away at a profit, you may decide to repurchase shares and set up a new risk hedge with a higher LEAPS put strike, and begin the process over, having taken profits from stock appreciation and options on the original risk hedge.

Proximity of Reversal Signals to Resistance and Support

The key to timing for both a long LEAPS and a short-term short option is the location of reversal signals and confirmation. These are found in the form of price, volume, moving averages and momentum; focusing primarily on price, numerous reversal signals can be located on the stock chart.

Fig. 9.2 Proximity of reversal signals to resistance or support

For example, the previously introduced resistance and support chart can be reviewed again, with strong reversal signals in the form of candlesticks. This marked-up chart is shown in Fig. 9.2.

Each of the short-term trends is identified clearly with reversal signals. This makes timing of entry and exit reliable and will improve your successful timing averages. The key candlestick signals were:

1. *Bullish doji star* appearing at the end of a strong and rapid downtrend. This is confirmed by the unusually long lower shadow on the second day of the signal, indicating a likely bullish reversal.
2. *Three white soldiers*, further confirming that a bullish reversal was underway.
3. *Bearish engulfing* at the top of another short-term trend, signaling a likely end to the trend (which did not occur until three weeks later).
4. *Bearish harami cross* appearing within a newly established trading range and appearing very close to resistance. The proximity confirms the reversal.
5. *Bullish harami*, found with price moving below support with a long black session. After a brief delay, the expected bullish reversal took price back all the way to resistance.
6. *Bearish meeting lines*, in close proximity to resistance.

The proximity of reversal signals only strengths them; in fact, when reversal signals appear within the range itself, they are likely to be false signals. Proximity to resistance or support is the key to well-timed reversals. This is especially true for short-term, short calls or puts used to pay for the LEAPS premium.

Historical Volatility

There are two versions of volatility. *Implied volatility* is the estimated future risk of the option itself, and this relies on estimates. It is of questionable value; options are also called *derivatives* because their value is derived from the underlying security. For this reason (in addition to the fact that calculating future volatility is impossible), the options trader will see more reliable results when using *historical volatility*.

This is based on history and is precise, versus implied volatility and its dependence on estimates about the future. Historical volatility is calculated by statistically calculating the standard deviation between the current price and the average price of the underlying. The greater this deviation, the higher the historical volatility.

Because historical volatility calculates how far current price has moved away from the average of price, it is a measurement of risk. An initial reaction among options traders might be to avoid high volatility for that reason. Why accept higher risk?

However, one primary reason for using installment strategies is to manage risk. When you purchase a LEAPS call, you freeze the strike price for possible future purchase. When you own stock and purchase a LEAPS put, you eliminate all market risk below the strike. The hedge against market risk is most effective for higher volatile (higher risk) underlying securities.

Higher volatility also leads to richer options premium, meaning that the installment income is likely to reduce the net basis of the LEAPS down to zero more rapidly, due to high volatility. However, for using short-term short positions to create installment payments, you must be careful to avoid exercise risk; this means exiting or rolling positions if the underlying moves against the option and threatens to move the short position in the money.

Volatility analysis helps you to manage the trade. The best method for making this judgment is to rely on the visual representation of historical volatility found in Bollinger Bands. In Chap. 4, a discussion and demonstration of this included not only the bands as representations of resistance and support, but the added value of the t-line to identify short-term trends.

When Bollinger Bands is studied with volatility in mind, the nature of risk based on price behavior becomes visible. This was illustrated in Chap. 4. If the default of two standard deviations is increased to three, the exceptional price behavior moments are easily observed in Bollinger Bands. It is unusual for price to ever move outside of three standard deviations. One example of a brief extreme move is shown in Fig. 9.3.

On May 4 and 7, price moved in an extreme manner, closing below the lower Bollinger Bands. This unusual move signaled that an immediate bullish

Fig. 9.3 Bollinger Bands and historical volatility

reversal was about to occur. Price rarely remains outside of three standard deviations for more than two or three sessions. The almost certain immediate reversal was also signaled and confirmed by three additional signals.

First was the extraordinary price gap, moving price down 12 points, from $59 to $47. Second was the volume spike, which is a move well above the average daily volume, which then returns without pause back to more typical volume levels. Third was the movement of the relative strength index (RSI) index below the oversold level. When these three signals, added to the price moving below lower Bollinger, are considered together, a bullish reversal is certain. This occurred with price next moving from the low of $44 per share to $50 in only nine sessions.

Volume spikes are revealing, often accompanying strong reversals. For purposes of observing and calculating historical volatility, price spikes are also important. Because they are exceptional, they should be excluded from a calculation of volatility. A principle in statistics observes that values within a field that are not typical (such as spikes) will distort averages and should be excluded from a calculated average.

Fig. 9.4 Price spike

For example, in Fig. 9.4, a price spike was found in the form of an island cluster. This is a brief number of sessions trading outside of the established price range, characterized by gaps before and after. The spike then concludes, and price reverts to a more typical range. In this example, the failed breakout above resistance marked this spike. The move of RSI above the overbought index value also confirmed the likelihood that the breakout would fail.

The price spike can take many forms, most often with the symptom of gaps between two price levels. Also look for confirmation in momentum or in volume spikes. The unusual price behavior most often leads to immediate reversal; in selecting short options, timing is favorable when the extreme price spike is seen.

Combining the Alternatives

Armed with a short list of strong technical signals, a trader may time entry and exit of trades to improve the instances of profit and reduce those of loss. Beyond the one-to-one short position versus LEAPS, the strategy can be expanded even more. Converting a single LEAPS position into a straddle, strangle or spread provides a two-direction hedge.

For example, a straddle is created by simultaneously opening a LEAPS call and a LEAPS put at the same strike. An example involves the purchase of 200 shares of Helmerich & Payne (HP) on February 9, 2018. The price per share was $68.29 and, adding trading fees, the total invested was $13,664. Two months later on April 4, a two-direction hedge was opened based on a long straddle. January 2019 options were selected at the 65 strike. This selection was based on the price per share on April 4.

The LEAPS 65 call was at an ask price of 7.40 and with trading fees, cost a total of $745. The LEAPS 65 put had an ask price of 8.40 and cost $845. Total invested was $1590. In less than two months, the sale of 15 short option positions generated $1905 in net profits, exceeding the required offset by $315. The full history of these trades is shown in Table 9.1.

Trades consisted of 11 covered calls and 4 uncovered puts. With overall profits from options of $1905 versus the cost of LEAPS long options of $1590, the net basis of both call and put were reduced to zero by June 15, 2018. With seven months remaining before expiration of the LEAPS contracts, the trader was in an enviable position. Any movement in the underlying either above or below $65 per share would create a net profit in one of the options.

Table 9.1 Two-direction hedge, Helmerich & Payne

Description of the trade	Purchase Date	Amount ($)	Sale Date	Amount ($)	Profit ($)
1 call, Apr 20, 67.50 strike, bid 1.90	4/9/18	120	4/5/18	185	65
1 put, Apr 20, 67.50 strike, bid 0.80	4/16/18	20	4/5/18	75	55
1 call, May 18, 70 strike, bid 5.10	4/24/18	456	4/18/18	505	49
2 puts, May 18, 67.50 strike, 1.75 bid	5/4/18	186	5/1/18	344	158
3 calls, May 18, 67.50 strike, bid 3.10	5/8/18	337	5/4/18	923	586
2 calls, May 18, 70 strike, bid 1.10	5/9/18	166	5/9/18	214	48
3 calls ratio write, Jun 15, 70 strike, bid 3.80	5/18/18	1093	5/16/18	1133	40
2 calls, Jun 15, 70 strike, bid 3.60	5/23/18	486	5/18/18	714	228
2 calls, Jun 15, 67.50 strike, bid 4.10	5/24/18	726	5/23/18	814	88
2 calls, Jun 15, 70 strike, bid 1.85	5/25/18	216	5/24/18	364	148
2 puts, Jun 15, 67.50 strike, bid 1.90	5/30/18	306	5/25/18	374	68
2 calls, Jun 15, 70 strike, bid 0.90	5/31/18	126	5/25/18	174	48
2 calls, Jul 20, 70 strike, bid 1.65	6/4/18	236	5/31/18	324	88
2 calls, Jun 15, 65 strike, bid 1.35	6/4/18	136	6/4/18	264	128
2 puts, Jun 15, 62.50 strike, bid 0.85	6/7/18	56	6/5/18	164	108
Total		4666		6571	1905
1 call, Jan 2019, 65 strike, ask 7.40	4/4/18	745			−745
1 put, Jan 2019, 65 strike, ask 8.40	4/4/18	845			−845
Net profit (56 days)		6256		6571	315

Source: Net trades executed by the author

The LEAPS call set up the potential for a purchase at some point of an additional 100 shares at $65 per share, no matter how high the underlying price moved. For example, if HP's price moved to $80 per share, buying 100 shares at $65 would set up an immediate profit of $1500. As an alternative the trader could sell the call for a profit of at least $1500 in intrinsic value.

If the price moved below $675 per share by expiration, the LEAPS put could be exercised and 100 shares sold at $65 per share. For example, if the underlying price declined to $57 per share, exercise at $65 eliminated the market price of depreciated stock. If the trader wanted to keep shares, selling the put for a profit of at least $800 ($65−$57) would offset the depreciation in the underlying price.

Shares originally were purchased for $68.29. The strike of 65 is $329 below the original basis. As shown in the table, as of June 15, 2018, the two-direction hedge had not only paid for the LEAPS options but created an additional $315 in net profits. This offsets nearly all of the net difference between original price per share and the LEAPS strikes.

A variation of the two-direction risk hedge is the synthetic stock trade. This is among the best forms of leverage a stock investor can use. The *synthetic stock* trade employs options to mirror price movement in the underlying stock, moving point for point with the underlying price.

For the investor, this means that for no added risk (beyond stock ownership), shares of stock can be controlled and exploited, even without owning shares directly.

There are two types of synthetic stock positions, long and short. The synthetic long stock trade combines a long call and a short put, with the same strike and expiration. The net cost will be close to zero, and perhaps even yield a small net credit. This strategy is suitable when you believe the underlying price is likely to rise. Entry is best timed at the bottom of a price swing. The ideal timing is when price has gapped below support. If you employ Bollinger Bands to identify dynamic resistance and support, time a synthetic long stock trade for price movement under the lower band. The extreme case is when price moves even lower, below Bollinger's lower band based on three standard deviations rather than the default of two standard deviations. In this situation, the likelihood of price rebounding is at its highest.

The synthetic short stock is a bearish alternative to shorting stock or entering another options-based strategy. Like the long synthetic, this strategy costs little or nothing to open; but it enables you to control shares of stock without added risk. Timing is best when the underlying has moved above support and a retracement or reversal is expected.

As an alternative to selling single options to pay for a LEAPS position, the synthetic has both positive and negative attributes. The greatest negative is that it provides no immediate credit to pay down the long-term option's cost. You rely on profitability in the synthetic to produce profits. In comparison, the single short option can be opened week after week and produce consistent profits over the long term. Another negative is the risk factor, especially for the synthetic short stock trade. Because it includes a short call, it is high risk if you do not own the underlying. If that short call is uncovered, the exercise risk should not be ignored.

This risk can be mitigated by timing the synthetic short stock trade at the top of the price swing and focusing on short-term expiration. The risk is further removed if you own 100 shares of the underlying for each synthetic position opened. As a variation of the risk hedge, the synthetic short stock eliminates all risk below the strike because the synthetic position does not cost much and may even be opened at a small net credit.

The risk for the synthetic long stock is quite low. It provides a long call for little or no cost, because its premium is paid by the premium of the short put. At the same time, the short put risk is low, with market risk identical to that of a covered call. As a variation of the contingent purchase installment, the synthetic long stock trade is attractive. It may also solve the problem of uncertainty. At some moments in the cycle of stock price behavior, you will not be sure that the underlying price will move as expected. The synthetic alternative may be more attractive at such times than either a short call or a short put.

An example: the value of MMM as of the close on June 11, 2018, was $205.12 per share. Rounding to $205 and using 205 strikes, synthetic long or short positions could be opened. An interesting aspect of the synthetic positions is that time is not as crucial as it is for single options.

In the case of opening short puts or short calls, the time to expiration determines how rapidly time decay takes place. However, because the synthetic position is an offset between a long and a short position, the time decay factor is not as important in the selection of strikes. In most instances, the synthetic long stock will set up a net debit, and the synthetic short position will set up a small credit. The 46-day expirations for MMM based on 205 strikes demonstrate this (with adjustments assuming $5 trading fees):

<u>Synthetic long stock, July 27 expiration</u>
Buy 205 call, ask 6.40 = $645
Sell 205 put, bid 5.30 = $525
      Net debit = $120

Synthetic short stock, July 27 expiration
Buy 205 put, ask 5.60 = $565
Sell 205 call, bid 6.15 = $610
Net credit = $45

The outcome for both positions is shown in Table 9.2.

The net difference between synthetic options and stock price is the same at each price point. At expiration of any price, the difference in profit or loss between options or stock will be identical to the net debit or credit of the synthetic position.

For the synthetic long stock, increase in the underlying will be matched by an increase in the synthetic position point for point (adjusted by the $120 debit for opening the position). If the underlying price declines, the synthetic position also declines point for point, adjusted by the $120 debit. The market risk for the synthetic long stock is identical to the market risk for purchasing 100 shares of stock.

Table 9.2 Synthetic stock trades

Underlying price ($)	Long 205 call ($)	Short 205 put ($)	Net options ($)	Stock profit or loss ($)
Synthetic long stock				
195	−645	−475	−1120	−1000
197	−645	−275	−920	−800
199	−645	−75	−720	−600
201	−645	125	−520	−400
203	−645	325	−320	−200
205	−645	525	−120	0
207	−445	525	80	200
209	−245	525	280	400
211	−45	525	480	600
213	155	525	680	800
215	355	525	880	1000
Synthetic short stock				
195	435	610	1045	−1000
197	235	610	845	−800
199	35	610	645	−600
201	−165	610	445	−400
203	−365	610	245	−200
205	−565	610	45	0
207	−565	410	−155	200
209	−565	210	−355	400
211	−565	10	−555	600
213	−565	−190	−755	800
215	−565	−390	−955	1000

The opposite applies to the synthetic short stock trade. As the underlying price declines, the net synthetic short stock position gains, and as the underlying price rises, the synthetic position loses. In both long and short versions of this strategy, the change in the underlying is mirrored by either positive or negative changes in the synthetic position.

Selection of long or short versions of a synthetic strategy rely on your perception of the underlying and whether it is likely to advance or decline in the near term. This is true for all options trades, of course, and the timing of a trade is crucial. Synthetics often work best in times of uncertainty. A clear signal of a stock's trading cycles and trends makes it easy to select single short options. However, in the case of MMM, the next direction was not clear, as shown in Fig. 9.5.

The history of MMM revealed a loss of 50 points in the stock price over four months. Resistance declined over that time from $255 per share to $205 per share. However, since the beginning of June, price had reversed and for the first time since late January, moved above upper Bollinger Band.

This could be interpreted as a signal of a reversal and the start of a new bullish trend. Or it could be seen as the end of a short-term bullish swing trade and likely retracement back below the declining trend line. This uncertainty could indicate the best timing for a synthetic stock trade.

Fig. 9.5 Synthetic stock trades

Multiple Increments and Combinations

The short side of the installment strategy can be modified in many ways. Using single-option short positions to pay for single-option LEAPS positions is the most basic of strategies; however, it is also possible to open more than one LEAPS position and then rely on the same multiples of short positions to create installments.

This increases risk in several ways. Using short calls (especially uncovered) expands exercise risk, and the same exercise risk may also apply to short puts. When multiple short positions are opened, the risk increases. Another way the risk is increased is through the threat that the LEAPS positions might not be paid down to a zero basis before expiration. In this case, the shortfall represents a net loss (between the cost of the LEAPS positions and the income from short-term short positions). A well-chosen situation is likely to not face this risk, but it exists nonetheless and should not be overlooked.

The use of multiple LEAPS and short-term positions also creates advantageous situations. As a swing trading strategy, the multiple positions can be matched to the number of LEAPS positions opened. For example, with two long-term LEAPS set up, you can trade two short calls, two short puts or one short position of each.

Another variation of multiples includes setting up multiple short-term expirations. In most situations, remaining focused on the shortest possible expiration makes the most sense because time decay is most accelerated in the option's final week. However, when premium is exceptionally rich, using one-week and two-week expirations can vastly expand the overall income from short option timing. By "leap frogging" the options, profits can be looked on a regular basis and strikes altered based on movement of the underlying. Based on direction of price movement, you also can switch back and forth between short calls and short puts when more than one position is opened.

Even without adding extra LEAPS positions, you can set up a more aggressive program of short options. Even with only one long-term option open, you can use expanded expiration and strike to create ratio writes using either calls or puts. This expands potential income, but also adds greater exercise risk. With the risk in mind, it is sensible to select longer term options with greater buffer zones between strike and current price of the underlying. This reduces premium income, but also reduces exercise risk.

In all these situations, it also makes sense to monitor positions every day. If the underlying begins trending in an unexpected direction and short options approach or move into the money, it could make sense to close and take a small loss, or to roll forward to a later expiration as well as a more advantageous strike (higher for short calls or lower for short puts).

A final possibility with the use of short options is the ultimate risk hedge, setting up both a bullish and a bearish shorty position. This is accomplished with straddles, strangles or spreads, and with risk varying based on whether underlying shares are held at the time a position is opened.

The bullish and bearish combination is attractive because one side or the other will benefit with price movement, and with little or no price movement, time decay sets up profit potential on both sides of the hedge. For example, setting up a net credit with a short-term butterfly spread or condor spread could produce profits while also holding risk in check. However, multiple-part options strategies are complex and demand constant monitoring.

It makes sense with all short positions to monitor every day that they remain open. However, a trade with as many as four separate strikes (e.g. butterfly or condor) will involve both bullish and bearish positions and exercise threat for half of those positions at any time. This presents a more complex dimension to the relatively simple installment strategy based on single options trades.

Notes

1. Hoffland, David L. (1967). The folklore of Wall Street. *Financial Analysts Journal*, Vol. 23, No. 3, pp. 85–88.
2. Passarelli, Dan (2011). *The Market Taker's Edge: Insider Strategies from the Options Trading Floor*. New York: McGraw-Hill Education, p. 7.

10

Expanding the Strategies

The installment strategies (contingent purchase and risk hedge) by themselves offer tremendous advantages to traders. By fixing the price for future purchase or eliminating market risk below a selected strike, you can overcome the risks normally associated with short-term trading (fast time decay and worthless expiration) as well as with long-term trading (high cost and unresponsive premium movement with improved intrinsic value). These problems have inhibited many options traders from exploring the potential for these forms of hedging.

The initial choice of long or short also inhibits many options traders. The installment strategy requires application of both long and short options, and for many this presents excessive risk. However, this attitude presents a model risk rather than a market risk. The model risk relates to attitudes toward strategies; for example, a trader may consider writing options as too risky, and will tend to favor long options. This model has nothing directly to do with the better understood market risk. In fact, effective trading based on long and short

> options involve the asymmetry between buying and writing, in that the option buyer has liability limited to the amount invested but the option writer is exposed to the risk of losses that can greatly exceed the initial premium received. Not surprisingly, the public prefers to buy options rather than to write them.[1]

To think in terms of both long and short strategies, traders need to overcome the aversion to short risk. With the expansion of strategies, even the most conservative trader will be able to accomplish what every trader wants:

control over risk through selective combinations and advanced strategies. These are designed to overcome, avoid and eliminate risk even beyond the hedging with the basic installment strategy. This chapter explains several of these techniques and strategies as they apply to installment positions.

Rolling Techniques

The first topic is not a strategy, but an exercise-avoidance technique. Rolling an in-the-money (ITM) short option forward to later expiration is a common practice among traders, but it is not bulletproof and does not ensure that the problems intended to be avoided are avoided.

There are several forms of rolling. All are designed to close out a current short position prior to expiration when it is in the money or close enough to the money to represent risk worth avoiding. For example, a short call has a strike of 65 and the underlying has been advancing. Two days before expiration, the stock price is at $64.75. The holder of the short call is concerned that by expiration, the underlying price will have moved higher and the call will be in the money. In this situation a forward roll may be justified.

For calls, forward rolls can be executed to a later expiring position at the same strike. They can also be moved to a higher strike, so that future exercise potential occurs at a higher strike (and more net profit in the called-away stock). In some cases, traders will accept a small loss in exchange for trading today's strike for a higher strike. The theory in this is that giving up some net income is justified by the higher strike. It either prevents exercise or accomplished exercise in more favorable conditions. For example, a forward roll may set up a $1 debit but add 2.5 points to the strike.

A danger in rolling calls is that traders may easily lose sight of the adjusted basis in the new position. For example, a short call is rolled forward. The loss on the original call is 2 points. Exchanging this for a later expiring call yields 5 points and a net credit of 3 (5–2). However, the true net basis in the net short call is not 5 (premium received) but the adjustment when the loss is considered. Even though the new call has a premium of 5, its net basis with the loss is 3. In later deciding to buy to close the position, this is easily overlooked. For example, if the new position can be closed at a net cost of 3.75, it appears to be a 1.25-point net profit (5–3.75). However, because the true net basis in the net call is 3, this sets up a net loss of 0.75 (3–3.75).

Keeping track of net basis is essential to ensure that the later buy to close of the rolled position generates a true net profit and not a loss. Traders entering short positions must accept exercise as a possible outcome, and some traders have fallen into the trap of thinking exercise must be avoided at all costs. In fact, exercise may be the most reasonable outcome in many cases. For example, if the net credit for rolling forward is minimal, you must compare the small loss to the lost opportunity involved in keeping exposure to exercise for a longer period.

The same caveats apply to rolling short puts. These can be rolled to a later expiring put at the same strike, or to one with a lower strike. It may be rational to accept a small debit if a lower strike exceeds the level of the debit. However, short put writers must proceed with caution in the same way as small call writers. The dangers include:

1. Setting up an adjust basis but overlooking it when the new option is bought to close.
2. Keeping exposure open for too long a period, in exchange for minimal benefits.
3. Overlooking the acceptance of exercise as a viable outcome and comparing exercise to rolling to make a sound decision.

In any decision to roll out of one position and replace it with another, the overall purpose of opening short options should be the primary factor. The decision to accept exercise or to roll forward affects the outcome of the installment. The short positions are set up to pay for the LEAPS option. The two choices for ITM short options are: first, roll forward and extend the exposure period in exchange for a new net credit or, second, accept exercise and immediately offset the stock trade (shares are called away and immediately repurchased, or shares are put to you and immediately sold).

The problem with accepting exercise is one of net losses. If the point difference between strike and current price is significant, offsetting the stock trade results in a significant net loss equal to the point spread. However, rolling forward to avoid exercise avoids that loss but extends the period of exposure. During that period, you are not generating new premium income at the level required to pay for the LEAPS position.

Long Collars

The description of "long" and "short" collars is not heard often in options literature. This is because collars, by definition, combine a short covered call and a long put. Ownership of stock is assumed in this case, because the call is covered. In the context of an installment risk hedge, the "long" collar describes a replacement for a single long put.

The usual form of risk hedge is a long put opened to freeze market risk at the strike. Assuming you can pay for that LEAPS put by writing a series of short calls or puts between initiation date and put expiration, any movement in the stock below the put's strike is risk-free. For every point lost in the stock's price, a point is gained in intrinsic value of the put.

Replacing the single long put with a collar is one alternative to the opening of a long LEAPS put. Instead, opening a long put and a short call, both out of the money, provides the same potential: elimination of market risk in the event the stock price declines, at which point the short call will also expire worthless. In the alternative, if the underlying price rises before expiration, you would expect exercise. Or, to avoid exercise, the short call could be closed at a profit based on declining time value. It all comes down to what the net cost or benefit would be for a collar, opened in place of a long put.

For example, on July 19, 2018, IBM was trading at $149.50, up 5.20 points after beating earnings estimates after the previous day's close. You own 100 shares. The chart shows that the current price was approaching resistance with a large gap. Your concern is that the price will retrace and some of the current profits will be lost. The situation is shown in Fig. 10.1.

At this point, some traders will sell and take profits, and then if the price does decline, repurchase shares at a lower price. However, this is entirely speculative and easily could violate your standard—identifying, buying and keeping high-value investments and protecting them with the long put risk hedge.

Fig. 10.1 Long collar trade

As an alternative, you decide to open a collar based on options expiring June 21, 2019, which is 337 days in the future. With the underlying price at $14,950, you identify the following options to make up the long collar:

> Sell 150 call @ bid of 9.50 = $945 net
> Buy 145 put @ ask of 9.90 = $995 total
> Total net debit = $50

In this example, the net cost is only $50, and you have 337 days for the position to evolve. In comparison, just buying the LEAPS put at the same expiration would cost $995.

Possible outcomes include a rise in underlying price, a decline in underlying price or declining time value without substantial price movement.

A rise in the underlying price will take the covered call in the money. If the original purchase price of shares was lower than $149.50, exercise will create a net capital gain. This dollar value is equal to the call's strike of 150 minus the net debit of $50, or $149.50. However, early exercise is unlikely even for a covered call in the money; so there remains the possibility of being able to buy to close the call and profit from declining time value.

A decline in the underlying price is protected at the put's strike of 145, minus the $50 net debit for the collar, or a breakeven of $144.50. All risk below that level is offset by gains in the long put.

If the stock price does not move significantly over the next 337 days, both options will decline in value and may be closed at a net profit. This assumes that the short call falls more than the $50 net debit. In closing this position, the short side (call) needs to move only $50 to break even, and the long put can be allowed to expire worthless (or kept open in case the underlying price later declines below the put's strike).

The collar provides you the ability to control risk whether the underlying price moves in either direction or remains in a narrow price range. In the case of IBM, price had gapped higher to the point of resistance, and this presented the risk of a retracement to the downside. However, support was identified at approximately $137.50 per share, much lower than the put's strike. This means that the long put represents a worthwhile risk hedge, whereas the covered call offers the potential for a capital gain if the underlying stock is called away.

The "long collar" (replacement of a long LEAPS put with the collar) is a risk hedge in both directions, and it costs little or nothing to open. For these reasons, it is worth considering as an alternative to the long put version of the risk hedge.

Long-Term Long Straddles and Strangles

Another alternative applying to either the risk hedge or the contingent purchase position is replacement of a single long-term put with a combination in the form of a straddle or strangle.

These positions, consisting of a long call and a long put, will be expensive compared to single options. For this reason, it will be more difficult to cover the cost with single option contracts. This means that it will be necessary to open two short positions at a time. These may consist of two short calls, two short puts or one of each.

The problem with opening two short calls is that one will always be uncovered. For the trader willing to accept this risk acknowledging that rapid time decay probably favors the position, it requires acceptance of higher risks. A preferable approach would be to open one of each (a short straddle or strangle) or restrict trading to short puts only.

An example: Facebook (FB) lost many points in late July 2018. As of August 2, the chart revealed numerous signals, as shown in Fig. 10.2.

Fig. 10.2 Setup for long-term straddle or strangle

This chart showed what a trader would expect after such a large decline, in this case from $215 down to $175, a drop of 40 points in one day. In addition to the gap, a volume spike and relative strength index (RSI) move from overbought to oversold confirmed a possible reversal. However, the fate of FB at the time was not certain.

An argument could be made that the price level of $170 represented support also highlighted on the chart. This would forecast a bullish retracement or reversal. On that basis, a trader might be interested in setting up a long-term contingent purchase. However, the market news concerning FB was troubling at the time, so a further decline could also be possible.

Given this conflicting situation, a long-term straddle or strangle could have been a wise hedge. Rather than dealing with one long call or put offset by one short position, it would require opening two long-term positions and trading short options two at a time.

As of the close of the market on August 2, the stock price was $176.37. The following examples of long-term straddle and strangle LEAPS positions were noted for expirations of June 21, 2019, or 323 days (nearly 11 months) in the future:

Straddle

Long 175 call, ask 22.00, plus trading fees = $2205

Long 175 put, ask 16.25, plus trading fees = $1630

Total cost of a straddle = $3835

Strangle

Long 180 call, ask 19.55, plus trading fees = $1960

Long 175 put, ask 16.25, plus trading fees = $1630

Total cost of a straddle = $3590

These positions reveal the opportunity and the risk involved, but they do hedge risk in both directions. For the cost indicated, the straddle or strangle eliminates all risk above the call's strike and below the put's strike (assuming that in 323 days, the cost of these long options can be paid through the sale of short positions).

The possibility appears reasonable. As of August 2, the one-week options (expiring August 10) were priced as:

Close to the money

177.50 call, bid 2.02, less trading fees = $197

175 put, bid 1.85, less trading fees = $180

    Net credit = $377

Repeat 17 times, or once every 32 days = $3770 net profit

Out of the money

180 call, bid 1.14, less trading fees = $114

172.50 put, bid 1.07, less trading fees = $107

    Net credit = $221

Repeat 17 times, or once every 19 days = $3737 net profit

These one-week positions demonstrate that covering the cost of the LEAPS straddle or strangle would be possible. The idea is that, not knowing the future direction of the underlying but convinced that it presents a trading opportunity, the straddle or strangle provide breakeven points in a narrow range, and over 323 days.

On the upside and downside, the breakeven for the straddle is $175 per share. Once the LEAPS options are paid for, any movement away from $175 represents a net profit. The options can be sold to take profits. Or the calls can be exercised, and shares purchased at $175 per share. If the stock price moves below $175 per share and the trader is holding 100 shares, the put can be exercised to sell shares at $175.

For the straddle, the same rationale is made with one exception. On the upside, the breakeven price is $180 per share, and on the downside breakeven is $175.

Some traders will be discouraged from pursuing a strategy like this because the LEAPS cost is exceptionally high. But it remains possible to cover that cost and to realize a net profit whether the underlying price moves above or below the strike prices.

When is the hedge appropriate? Given the fact that the future direction of price movement cannot be known for the next 11 months, especially in the unusual situation FB was in as of the beginning of August 2018, traders could not be sure whether to be bullish or bearish. As a result, most traders would hesitate and avoid taking the risk. The straddle and strangle set up a two-way hedge, offering the potential for profit in the event of price movement in either direction.

Even if the price level remains unchanged for the next 11 months, the cost of the LEAPS straddle or strangle would be paid for through repetitive sales of one-week calls or puts. The strategy not only hedges for contingent purchase or sale; it hedges in both directions within the same strategy.

For many options traders, this is a novel idea. Traders tend to be optimistic, favoring bullish price movement over bearish. Consequently, many are taken by surprise when an underlying price declines. In reality, markets can (and do) move in either direction:

> Since the purchaser of options can make long-term capital gains on price swings regardless of either direction, he avoids the propensity to develop an upward bias toward the market and is continually on the alert for investments on the downside. In essence, better investment decisions are made because the market can be objectively looked upon as a two-way street.[2]

Short-Term Short Straddles, Strangles and Spreads

The opposite rationale also may be applied in a higher risk approach to rapidly paying for a long-term LEAPS. This applies to both the put-based risk hedge and the call-based contingent purchase.

The sale of short-term straddles, strangles and spreads is one way to rapidly pay for the cost of long LEAPS positions (either calls or puts), in exchange for accepting higher risks. Two major considerations apply in this approach. First, the use of short combinations requires twice as much collateral since two options are involved in the trade. Second, some of the options in these short positions will be in the money, especially for straddles (where one of the two options is always in the money unless the underlying remains exactly at the strike). With the strangle, a buffer zone is set up if both call and put are out of the money, and with the spread, a buffer zone also exists but any significant price movement can move one of the short sides in the money.

The use of the short straddle, strangle or spread requires timing so that time decay serves as the source for profits. The Friday prior to expiration is the most advantageous timing for opening these short positions, due to time decay in the five trading days between Fridays.

When short positions move in the money, time decay often offsets intrinsic value so that positions can be closed at a small profit. However, when the open options move far too far in the money and they are valued at a net loss, they can be rolled forward to avoid exercise. The problem with rolling is that this keeps exposure open longer; the profitability of the short-term option is in time decay and rolling delays this. However, as in the FB example, the completion of a short trade over 32 days adds flexibility to the schedule aimed at getting to break even before the long-term expiration date.

Covered Straddles and Strangles

A variation of the short-term and risk use of short straddles, strangles or spreads is the covered straddle or strangle. This is a combination of a covered call and an uncovered put, applicable when the trader owns 100 shares for each call opened.

The advantage in the covered straddle or strangle is that risks are reduced significantly. Because the call is covered, that side of risk is very low, and the uncovered put contains the same market risk, so even with two options involved, risk levels for the covered straddle are more manageable than for the uncovered straddle. For the strangle, risks are even lower because each side of the trade is out of the money.

The trade is applicable in situations when 100 shares are owned for each short straddle or strangle opened. Although this is probably most applicable to the risk hedge (eliminating downside risk for equity in the underlying), the covered straddle or strange also could be used when 100 shares are owned but the trader is considering purchasing more shares in the future.

For example, On August 2, 2018, Microsoft (MSFT) closed at $107.57. The chart shows the strong bullish trend underway since April, four months earlier, in Fig. 10.3.

Fig. 10.3 Chart for covered straddle or strangle

A trader holding 100 shares could hold two opinions in this situation. First, it seems likely that this strong performance could be the beginning of a longer term price advance. It would be desirable to purchase more shares at the current price. Second, the price could retreat, meaning the current paper profits would be lost.

Both opinions represent the perfect timing for a short-term covered straddle or strangle. The initial and continuing goal is to pay for a long-term LEAPS, whether this is a call, a put or a combination of both. By opening a short-term position to pay for that longer term long position, one-week options are ideal. As of the close on August 2, 2018, the following positions were available for expiration the following Friday, August 10:

Short straddle

107 call, bid 1.54, less trading fees = $149
107 put, bid 0.92, less trading fees = $87
Net credit = $236

Short strangle

108 call, bid 0.91, less trading fees = $86
106 put, bid 0.55, less trading fees = $50
Net credit = $136

The ideal outcome for either of these positions will be time decay that outpaces any underlying move above the strike of the call or below the strike of the put. As with any short position, ITM calls or puts can be rolled forward; but it is desirable to close positions and replace them the following week with new ones, representing aggressive generation of profits to speed up the process of covering the long LEAPS cost. The sooner that happens, the more flexibility in future actions (exercise or sale of the option).

Because Microsoft's price was strongly on the rise, it presents a dilemma for a trader holding shares. With no options in use, do you close and take profits or hold for further gains? With options, paper profits can be hedged, and all market risk removed. With the covered straddle or strangle, two considerable advantages are achieved: lower risk and more rapid payment of the long positions. At the same time, because both call and put have been opened, one side will be out of the money and can be closed at a profit or allowed to expire, and the other side will benefit from rapid time decay or can be rolled forward or bought to close at a small loss.

However, even with one side moving in the money, with only five days until expiration (Friday to Friday), chances are strong that even with intrinsic value acquired in the short option, time decay might outpace it, allowing the position to be closed at a small profit.

Straps and Strips

The use of weighted straddle can be employed in different ways, depending on whether it is opened as a long position or a short position. The weighted straddle comes in two varieties, the strap and the strip.

A strap consists of two calls and one put, all opened at the money. These options have the same strike and expiration, and it favors a bullish move. The position is expensive but could pay off handsomely if the underlying does move in the upward direction that the strap is intended to exploit.

For example, Chevron (CVX) was trading in a 7-point consolidation between $121 and $128 per share, between May and August 2018. The price per share at the close of August 3 was $124.05. This chart sets up the opportunity to trade a strap or a strip, as shown in Fig. 10.4.

Long Strap

An installment strategy could be opened in the form of a strap based on options expiring June 21, 2019, or 322 days in the future. The closest strike to the money was the 125 option:

Fig. 10.4 Chart for strap or strip trade

125 calls, ask 8.15: 2 contracts plus $6 trading fee = $1,636
125 put, ask 10.45 plus $5 trading fee =   1,050
     Total cost = $2,686

To offset this LEAPS strap, sell one-week at the money (ATM) options in the same configuration:

124 calls, bid 1.12: 2 contracts less $6 trading fee = $218
124 put, bid 1.03 less $5 trading fee =   98
     Net credit = $316

If a similar trade were entered nine times, it would pay for more than the cost of the LEAPS strap:

$$\$316 * 9 = \$2844$$

That works out of one trade every 36 days. Considering that this strategy is intended to work on a week-to-week basis, that provides a comfortable margin to pay for the long strap.

Long Strip

Another method favors a bearish long-term trend. The strip consists of two puts and one call opened at the same strike and expiration, all options at the money. A similar setup reveals that the strip would be paid for with a comfortable schedule. Based on the same long-term expirations as those used for the strap, an installment strategy would consist of options expiring June 21, 2019, or 322 days in the future. The closest strike to the money was the 125 option:

125 puts, ask 1,045: 2 contracts plus $6 trading fee = $2,096
125 call, ask 8.15 plus $5 trading fee =   820
     Total cost = $2,916

To offset this LEAPS strip, sell one-week ATM options in the same configuration:

124 puts, bid 1.55 : 2 contracts less $6 trading fee = $304
124 call, bid 0.65 less $5 trading fee =   60
    Net credit = $364

If a similar trade were entered eight times, it would pay for the cost of the LEAPS strap:

$$\$364 * 8 = \$2912$$

That works out of one trade every 40 days. As with the strap, the intention for the short side of the installment is to enter a trade each week. With a 40-day period the minimum required, this is not a difficult goal to reach.

Considering that both the strap and the strip are so nicely configured in this example, it would make sense to reduce short-side risks by building in a buffer zone. Selecting different strikes allows for underlying price movement with a lower exercise risk; this means the need to roll forward to avoid exercise will not be a problem as many times as it could be when all the short options are opened at the money.

Either of these strategies can convert an otherwise one-to-one strategy into a highly profitable hedge with expanded possibilities. If you are correct about direction of underlying price movement, your future profit is earned on a two-to-one basis. You have two calls in the strap, meaning those calls gain two points of intrinsic value for every upward point in the underlying; you have two points in the strip, so that those puts gain two points in intrinsic value for every point of decline in the underlying.

If you are mistaken about the direction of underlying price movement, nothing is lost. You pay for the long positions through short offsets, so that before expiration your basis is zero. The one option in the money can be sold or exercised in the same way as the one-to-one variety of either contingent purchase or risk hedge.

As expiration approaches for the long side, the choices are also expanded. For a strap and appreciated stock, you can exercise both and buy 200 shares at a price below market value. You can sell the two calls and gain intrinsic value (and also sell the put). Or you could exercise one call and sell the other. For a strip, the same range of choices is available. Exercise both and sell 200 shares at the strike, above market value. Sell both and take profits. Or exercise one and sell one.

Choices are desirable, of course. The strap and strip not only hedge the underlying price even with many points of movement. They also hedge the direction of price movement.

Multiple Option Contracts

Variation of the installment strategy is not limited to combined calls or puts, long versus short, or long term versus fast expiration. The strategy can also be expanded to include multiple contracts. What works in a one-to-one approach also works in five-to-five or more.

Some efficiency is gained in opening multiple positions. The trading fee per contract declines as the number of opened positions increases. However, in today's low-commission world, the issue of trading fees is not as crucial as it was in the past. As online brokers compete for business, trading fees continue to decline. The small advantage gained in reduced trading costs is of little significance.

Potential disadvantages are more serious, so using multiple contracts should be approached with caution and astute awareness of risks. The short-side risk for a single contract demands careful management to avoid exercise, decide when or if to roll, and even the most basic selection of a strike and creation of a buffer zone (between strike and current price of the underlying). The buffer zone is a risk management concept, in which lower premium credits are accepted in exchange for lower risk.

The risk applies in both long and short positions. For long options, the risk is that time decay will outpace intrinsic value, or the option will never move in the money, so no intrinsic value is gained. For the short position, the risk is that the option will move in the money and exercise risk accumulates as the price moves against the trader.

In considering multiple contracts (with the same strike and expiration), the risk rises with the number of options opened. Consequently, the risk for ten short options is ten times greater than for one option.

Another inhibiting factor when using multiple short options is the collateral issue. Collateral must be maintained in the margin account for uncovered short options; this requirement will be greater as the number of contracts increases. This is offset when short positions are accompanied with long positions, so that in a spread, for example, the collateral is based on a net difference between strikes.

Variations in multiple contracts are also possible:

1. *Vary the expiration date.* The basic calendar spread is part of the installment strategy. However, separate expirations can also be used for the short offsets. For example, you open five LEAPS positions and plan to pay for them by selling short-term options. Rather than limiting this to the next closest expiration, open two options expiring in one week and three more expiring in

two weeks. This expands the period of exposure but also increases premium income. As shorter term positions expire they can be replaced with new options expiring even later.
2. *Use multiple strikes.* The use of buffer zones reduces exercise risk. The same benefit can be expanded to offset multiple LEAPS positions with two or more strikes. This changes overall net income received for opening short options; it is also possible to combine short calls and short puts. For example, with five LEAPS positions open, five separate strikes can be used: an ATM call and one calls at each of the next higher strikes, and two of the lower strike puts also opened. This spread of strikes produces advantageous outcomes on one side or the other, and at the same time, ITM options can be closed or rolled.
3. *Combine different expirations and strikes.* The multiple expiration and multiple strike approach can be used together. Setting up diagonal exposure periods and buffer zones adds variety to the short offsets for long LEAPS positions and leads to selection of some options to close or roll, and others to allow to expire.
4. *Use different multiples on long and short sides.* The short side itself can be weighted by creation of ratio call or put writes. For example, with five LEAPS positions, sell seven calls or puts (or a combination of both). This 7:5 ratio (or, 1.4 to 1) represents 71% coverage or a combined 5–5 coverage with two uncovered options in the ratio.

* * *

Many possible combinations and variations are possible, limited only by the trader's imagination. The advantage in the installment strategy is its flexibility. The use of calls with puts, long with short, and long term with short term, provides potential for variations to increase net income while managing risk, and setting up degrees of hedging to improve long-term portfolio management.

Notes

1. Green, T., & Figlewski, S. (1999). Market Risk and Model Risk for a Financial Institution Writing Options. *The Journal of Finance, 54*(4), 1465–149.
2. Snyder, Gerard L. (1967). A Look at Options. *Financial Analysts Journal, 23*(1), 100–103.

11

Managing Potential Losses

The installment strategy combines long and short positions and combines long-term expiration and short-term expiration. This does not have to be a complex of time-intensive process, but it does demand monitoring. Many losses investors and traders experience occur because they do not check the status of their positions daily, notably short positions, and may not take profits when they are available.

This chapter describes the risks faced by those using the installment strategy. Too many promises may be made to options traders of "guaranteed profits" or "sure-fire risk-free trading" with a system. This promise is irresponsible because no system works all the time. Even with the best signals and most thought-out timing of trades, matters can go wrong. In the next chapter, recovery strategies in those times are explored.

To institutional investors, risk is perceived as either hedging or speculation. The same criteria should be applied by individuals to better understand their own risk profiles:

> Risk management that reduces return volatility is frequently termed hedging, and risk management that increases return volatility is called speculation … Derivatives users have consistently argued that regulators' concerns about the dangers of derivatives (i.e., speculation) are misplaced. They contend that the direct and indirect costs of "excessive" regulation will reduce derivatives usefulness.[1]

The argument that more regulation is not needed may be hollow. During the 2008–2009 period, the many institutional abuses of derivatives came to light and led to many large bankruptcies. The cited article, written seven years before the meltdown that began in 2008, did not anticipate how widespread the devastation was going to be, nor did it even imagine the extent of abuses tied to derivatives risk.

For institutions, the need for regulation and oversight is clear; for individuals, a more immediate concern, even in a conservative portfolio, is how to recover from unexpected losses in single trades. A more pervasive level of speculation is not likely to include strategies for installment purchase or sale of options.

Before considering how to recover from a trade moving against you, a first step should be to recognize the steps you can take before and during the trade to avoid the problem altogether.

Short Positions at Risk

The long LEAPS side of the installment poses a risk. If it is not paid for by short positions, *and* if the underlying does not move in the money, the LEAPS could expire worthless. This potential loss is very real; but as examples in previous chapters have revealed, the possibility that the LEAPS can be paid for between entry and expiration is very likely. For that reason, the long option risks are minor in comparison to risks of the open short positions.

As a first step, the risks between short calls and short puts should be recalled. There are three distinct classifications of short options, each with completely different risk considerations.

Covered Calls

The lowest risk selection is the covered call. If the selected strike is higher than the basis in the underlying, and if one call is matched with 100 shares of stock, there is no realistic risk of loss on the upside. If the call ends up in the money, 100 shares are called away at a profit. A trader earns three forms of profit in this case: capital gain on the stock, option premium and dividends.

In the downside, risks are of more concern. If the underlying declines below the net basis, a paper loss occurs. The net basis is the price paid for 100 shares, minus premium received for selling the covered call. For example, a trader paid $48 per share and sold a call for 3 ($300). The net basis is $45 per share, the initial cost minus premium.

If the underlying has declined below this net basis, a sale of stock would be at a loss. Traders usually end up waiting out this situation and hoping the underlying price will rebound and return to its original level; but there is no way of knowing how long this will take. Writing a new covered call may require selection of a strike below the basis in stock. This is not acceptable because exercise would result in a net loss. Perhaps the most realistic alternative is to sell an uncovered put. The risk of exercise would mean acquiring more shares at the strike, which means you must be willing to increase your holdings in the underlying in that event.

Uncovered Calls

A much higher risk alternative is writing uncovered calls. In theory, upside risk is unlimited; if the underlying price moves far above the strike, the call writer loses the net difference between strike and current price at the time of exercise. Uncovered calls are likely to be written by a trader entering an installment in the form of a contingent purchase.

Writing uncovered calls at strike above the strike of a LEAPS call makes sense if possible, because using the LEAPS call to satisfy exercise would involve buying at a lower strike and selling at a higher strike. However, the cost of the LEAPS premium is likely to create a net loss in such a trade.

Uncovered calls are alternated with uncovered puts by a trader in the contingent purchase trade. In the ideal timing of each, an uncovered call is opened when the underlying price has spiked to a high point. Most favorable is a move above resistance, especially with a price gap. The likelihood of retracement is highest at this proximity. Resistance can be measured by the traditional straight line above price, or by the more reliable and accurate upper Bollinger Band.

If the underlying price declines, the uncovered call can be closed at a profit or allowed to expire. The strategy, like all short options, relies on rapidly declining time value. For this reason, two requisite conditions should be observed when opening the uncovered call. First, it should occur when price of the underlying has gapped above resistance. Second, when possible a buffer zone should be set between current price and the call's strike. This allows you to buy to close the position in the event of a move toward the money.

Uncovered Puts

The third possibility is the uncovered put. This has the same market risk as the covered call, so it is a relatively conservative trade. This does not mean there is no risk, but it does provide greater rolling flexibility than the covered call. Without needing to be concerned about underlying exercise, a roll can be made to any strike that could be profitable.

Alternating the call and the put in a short position should follow the same proximity rules. The best time to open an uncovered put is when the underlying has moved below support. The ideal condition is when the underlying price gaps lower, setting up the conditions in which upside retracement is most likely. The support level can be measured as a straight line or as the lower Bollinger Band.

Both resistance and support can be further and more accurately measured when Bollinger Band is overlaid with the t-line, the eight-day simple moving average of price. The two work very well together to identify channels and to mark the borders of the trading range.

When the underlying price is moving upward, resistance is represented by the upper band and support is marked by a rising t-line. When the underling price is moving downward, resistance is marked by a declining t-line and support is seen in the lower band. This system if combining these two signals is the most effective system for tracking price within the trading range.

It not only provides a clear picture of the trading range; it also clearly shows when the trend is beginning to turn in the opposite direction. A violation of either Bollinger Band signals likely reversal (above the upper or below the lower). When price crosses the t-line, it also signals likely trend reversal. The general rule is that if price is below the t-line and then crosses above and closes there for two days, it is a signal of the end of a bearish trend and beginning of a bullish reversal. When the price is above the t-line and crosses below, closing there for two days or more, it marks the end of a bullish trend and the beginning of a bearish one.

All the short positions—covered call, uncovered call and uncovered put—contain degrees of risk. However, by coordinating timing with the signals developed on the price chart, timing is vastly improved.

The Advantage of Time Decay

Short positions are strategically set up to exploit time decay. You want the most rapid decay possible, meaning the best timing is one week or less before expiration. Opening a short position on the Friday before expiration is the most advantageous timing. On average, options lose one-third of their remaining time value between Friday and Monday before expiration. This is because three calendar days pass, but only one trading day.

Time decay happens every day, including weekends and holidays. Timing should not be ignored. Opening positions requiring more time than one week has two shortcomings. First, although more premium is earned, you have a longer time of exposure. Second, time decay will not begin to occur as rapidly as desired until the last week. Although the premium for a two-week option will be higher, it invariably yields less income than the equivalent two weekly options.

Time decay is maximized when short opening is focused on the extremely short-term expiration. This, combined with the proximity between price and resistance/support, maximizes the potential for recurring profits. However, this is true only for those underlying stocks that offer weekly options.

Some stocks continue to offer only monthly options and do not offer weekly expirations. Although these might be viable candidates for installment strategies, they are not as likely to yield the kind of fast turnaround as those with weekly options.

Another consideration is short-term strike increments. The most desirable are those underlying with options available at every round dollar strike. In comparison, 2.5-point or 5-point strikes often frustrate traders when the underlying is in between the two closest possibilities. One-dollar strikes expand not only the possible strikes that can be opened, but also add flexibility in setting up a buffer between strike and current price.

Reducing Risk Exposure: Moneyness and Timing

The most successful short-side strategies are based on proximity of price to resistance or support. However, two additional attributes that add up to improved overall timing also must be added to the equation: moneyness and timing.

Moneyness is the relationship between the strike and the current underlying price. Some traders believe it is best to sell options slightly out of the money. If expiration comes up very soon, this can be a successful strategy. With only a few days remaining, chances are that time decay will exceed increases in intrinsic value—if the in-the-money (ITM) movement is not too rapid or for too many points. That is the problem; it is always possible that a short option will move in the money during the last few trading days in the option's life, and therefore traders must monitor the status every day. It does not require constant checking, but as expiration nears, it is prudent to check the status of any open short option and look for (a) opportunities to close at a profit or (b) threats of ITM movement and possible exercise.

Timing is closely related. In addition to paying attention to the number of days remaining until expiration, many traders believe that trades opened (or closed) at the time of the trading day will outperform the averages. Unfortunately, the selection of the best time for trades is a matter of opinion and, in studying this issue, the timing element is not consistent. There is no rationale for claiming that entering trades as soon as the market opens, right before it closes, or when most exchange people are at lunch, does not appear to offer a consistent advantage over the average values of options.

Timing within a trading day is not as reliable as the broader version of timing, selection of options expiration between one week and ten days. When combined with the consideration of moneyness of the option, timing is as important. The three attributes taken together—proximity, moneyness and timing—should all be coordinated and kept in mind when determining when to sell to open and when to buy to close.

Avoiding Ex-dividend Periods

Risk reduction is not limited to selection of the "best" call or put. It is not even limited to proximity, moneyness and timing. These are essential elements of picking the right option; but timing goes beyond these attributes and includes other matters that also could influence the value of options as well as exercise risk.

For any short call—whether covered or uncovered—the most likely time of exercise is the last trading day for any option in the money. If the position closes in the money, exercise will take place. If a trader on the other side holding a long call does not exercise, then automatic exercise will occur.

The Options Clearing Corporation (OCC) will automatically exercise any listed stock option that closes 0.01¢ or more in the money. For a short 50 call, when the underlying closes on the last trading day at $50.01 or higher, the call will be exercised. For a short 50 put, if the underlying closes on the last trading day at $49.99 or lower, the put will be exercised.

The second most likely time a short call will be exercised is immediately before ex-dividend date, a period known as cum-dividend ("with" dividend). On and after ex-dividend, a current quarterly dividend will not be earned. If the short call is in the money, it might be exercised in the days before ex-dividend date, but not in all cases. If the owner of a long call wants to execute a dividend capture strategy, and if the call is in the money, it could be exercised.

This brings up the dividend capture strategy:

> Holders of equity options are not entitled to receive the cash dividend paid to owners of the underlying stock, unless they exercise the calls prior to the ex-dividend date. Consequently, some owners of American-style call options have an

incentive to exercise immediately before the stock goes ex dividend. Essentially, exercise on the last cum-dividend day will be optimal if the value of the dividend exceeds the "time value" remaining in the option after the dividend. This is most likely to be the case for deep-in-the-money and short-term call options.[2]

This likelihood is important to installment strategy traders with short calls open in the week of ex-dividend. Dividend capture is a strategy with three parts:

1. Buy a call close to the money at some point before ex-dividend day, probably in the week preceding.
2. If the call moves in the money, the owner might exercise. However, this would occur only if the dividend is worth more than the premium of the call.
3. Sell the stock on ex-dividend date or later, assuming it can be sold at a profit.

The outcome of this strategy is that the trader moves in and out of the stock position in a very short period, as short-term as one day (exercise the call and buy stock the day before ex-dividend and then sell shares on ex-dividend date). This means the quarterly dividend is earned even though ownership of the stock took place in a very brief holding period.

For the trader executing an installment strategy, having the short call exercised creates both an inconvenience and a net cost. The call would be in the money, meaning the trader has a net loss equal to the difference between current price of the stock when the call was exercised and the strike.

Traders may be taken by surprise in the dividend capture strategy. An assumption may be that short positions are not vulnerable to early exercise when at or close to the money. This generally is true except for ex-dividend week.

The solution is to avoid setting up short calls close to the money that expire after or on ex-dividend date. During that week, either focus on short puts or delay making any trades. Even though not every short ITM call is exercised, the risk is great enough to avoid exercise.

Avoiding Earnings Week

Another week worth avoiding is the week when quarterly earnings are announced. The frequency of earnings surprises points to the risk of having short options open when a surprise might occur. The exaggerated underlying price movement often following makes the risks of short positions far worse and vulnerable to immediate exercise.

Traders should exercise caution in attempting to anticipate the direction of an earnings surprise. It is, by definition, not predictable, and many factors enter why earnings end up either above or below consensus estimates. As a rule,

> investors underreact to trends as a result of the gambler's fallacy. A classic example of this fallacy is when gamblers at a roulette wheel incorrectly believe that black is more likely to occur than red following a string of red draws. Intuitively, the gambler's fallacy is the belief that trends require immediate "balancing" by the opposite outcome.[3]

When applied to earnings surprises, a trader witnessing a string of negative surprises may expect a long overdue positive surprise, or vice versa. However, this is ill advised, yet another version of the gambler's fallacy. Traders will be wise to resist the temptation to think like gamblers and to act irrationally. The earnings surprise cannot be predicted, which is why waiting until after price reaction is set, and then exploiting exaggerated underlying price movement, is far wiser than trying to guess red or black in a game of roulette.

Misses do occur, and often. And even a miss in earnings of a few cents can cause a large price movement. In most cases, this exaggerated movement corrects itself within one to three days; but in the time that the movement remains, short options could gain considerable value, leading to the possibility of exercise and large losses for anyone with the open position.

The solution is to avoid opening options that do not expire until after the earnings announcement date. For example, on a Friday before expiration, avoid opening any options if earnings will be announced before the following Friday's expiration. Selecting a later expiration does not remove this risk; any short position that moves in the money after an earnings announcement is vulnerable, even if it does not expire for several weeks.

Any trader intent on reducing and controlling risks will be able to just avoid opening a trade during the week of earnings. However, there is another side to this. After earnings are announced and a surprise causes the underlying to move many points, the timing of a short trade is excellent. For example, a positive earnings surprise causes the underlying price to gap many points above its trading range. This is an excellent time to open a short call. The likelihood of retracement back toward the previous range is high, so this is the best timing to enter a trade. Once the short option becomes profitable, the position can be bought to close, and profits taken as part of the course of paying for a long-term LEAPS position.

When an earnings surprise is negative, the underlying price is likely to decline by many points. Expecting a retracement as soon as this price decline occurs timing is excellent for opening a short put. The price of the underlying is most likely to retrace and move up back into range. When this occurs, profit can be taken by buying to close the short puts.

An alternative could be to buy either calls or puts after an earnings surprise. However, given the endless problem of time decay and the theme of installment strategies—paying for long-term long options with short-term short options—taking a short-term long position may not be as profitable as the proposed short call or put.

In fact, the potential for fast profits after an earnings announcement is so great that traders may want to consider opening a ratio position. This means opening more short positions than they can cover, either with shares of the underlying or the long-term LEAPS. This can take several forms.

The covered call can be converted to a ratio write or a variable ratio write to increase income in the post-earnings announcement period. A short strap (two calls and one put) following a possible earnings announcement or a short strip (two puts and one call) also serve this purpose.

The advantage to timing of single options or ratio-based ones is in the fact that movement in the form of retracement could be rapid. For example, on August 1, 2018, Tesla (TSLA) announced earnings. The earnings per share were a negative surprise, missing estimates by 0.24¢. However, revenues beat estimates, reporting $400 billion, a positive surprise of $70 million. The Tesla chart in Fig. 11.1 showed the status of the stock as of the close of August 6.

A trader anticipating a retracement to offset this rise in price could open a short call, a ratio write or a short strap (two short calls and one short put). For example, a single short call with a strike close to current price. The four-day options expiring August 10 show that the $342.50 call was at a bid of 5.70 at the close of August 6. After trading fees, this would generate a net credit of $565. The underlying price was $341.99, or 0.51 points out of the money. With only four days remaining until expiration, this short call is advantageous.

A short strap is more aggressive. Opening two 342.50 calls at 5.70 bid generates a net credit of $1134. A single short put at the same strike was at a bid of 6.25, netting a credit of $620. The overall net credit would be $1754, with exposure for only four days. If timing is correct and all these options expire worthless (or lose value so they can be bought to close at a profit), the timing for a short strap is excellent. Time decay will be rapid. The 2-to-1 relationship between calls and puts mitigates the short call risk to the single contract.

Fig. 11.1 Positive earnings surprise

Most traders hesitate after earnings surprises. Even with knowledge about the likelihood of retracement after exaggerated price movement (e.g. 50 points in the case of Tesla), traders often are concerned that the price movement is not an exaggeration but a new trend. This is always possible. However, as a contrarian, a trader can exploit a 50-point price movement with well-timed short trades and generate profits in most cases.

When the price does not behave as expected, positions can be rolled forward or closed. In the example, with only four days remaining until expiration, time decay is likely to cause significant premium decline in all the options and could offset any intrinsic value that develops. However, taking the bold step of opening any short positions after an earnings surprise demands courage and conviction; the momentary instability of price adds create uncertainty in the minds of many traders.

The multiple-part short trade is significantly higher risk than a single-option trade. A short strap or strip generates healthy credits but, given the proximity of strike to underlying price, the market risk cannot be ignored. Therefore, the timing with earnings surprises is appealing; it reduces the overall risk because retracement is likely after exaggerated price movement.

Short-Term Expiration Advantages

Some traders, recognizing the risk of selling options, will object to the installment strategy. The risk is too high, as the argument goes. However, with all the requisite elements in place, risk is not specific to a strategy (such as selling options), but to the attributes, including four elements:

1. *Proximity of strike to price;* buffer zones are desirable because they allow the trader the ability to escape the position if the underlying moves toward the money.
2. *Proximity of price to trading borders;* when the underlying price moves above resistance or below support, chances for retracement are substantial.
3. *Timing of the trade.* A short call should be entered near the top of a swing trade; short puts should be opened near the bottom. Further timing issues involve post-earnings surprise entry to exploit retracement of exaggerated price movement.
4. *Accelerated time decay.* During the last week of the option's life, time decay is rapid. Between the Friday before expiration and the next trading day (Monday), options lose on average one-third of their remaining time value.

The four elements work together to reduce market risk. In comparison to these four points, when trades are opened at inopportune times, the market risks are increased. The short-term expiration works in most cases due to time decay. However, the other three elements improve the chances for profit. With this in mind, "risk" should not be thought of as belonging to strategies due to their mix of positions but varies with the attributes and timing of a trade.

Notes

1. Hentschel, L., & Kothari, S. (2001). Are Corporations Reducing or Taking Risks with Derivatives? *The Journal of Financial and Quantitative Analysis, 36*(1), 93–118.
2. Hao, J., Kalay, A., & Mayhew, S. (2010). Ex-Dividend Arbitrage in Option Markets. *The Review of Financial Studies, 23*(1), 271–303.
3. Loh, R., & Warachka, M. (2012). Streaks in Earnings Surprises and the Cross-Section of Stock Returns. *Management Science, 58*(7), 1305–1321.

12

Recovery Strategies

Every trader will experience losses. There are two mistakes traders make when this occurs. First, a trader may become fearful of additional losses and question the strategy undertaken, even when that strategy will succeed most of the time. This avoidance of further risk ignores the high potential of a conservative strategy and should be resisted.

Second, a trader may be tempted to offset a loss by increasing risk levels on future trades. This is often practiced by gamblers. When they lose a $20 bet, their next bet is $40, with the idea of winning back the loss. The problem here is that they are risking twice as much, and there is still a chance of losing even more—just for the chance of getting back what has been lost already. It makes more sense to accept the loss and continue applying a strategy you believe will result in winning more than losing.

Traders can easily become gamblers, even when they do not intend to. A "recovery strategy" does not demand that all losses be offset and erased in the next trade. It should be thought of as a system for identifying a winning strategy and taking steps to seek out those opportunities where the strategy has the best chance for success.

When your trade loses, it makes sense to get out early and accept a small loss, rather than waiting in the hope that the price will turn around and erase the loss. Recovery of a smaller loss is easier than one for a large loss. Too many traders allow their ego to get in the way. If a loss is intolerable and unacceptable to a trader, the program has been written: more losses will occur if the trader is inflexible.

After suffering a loss, recovery can come in many forms. Remember the starting point: once you see that a trade is losing, get out as soon as possible to keep the loss to a minimum. Then the next strategy intended to recover losses is easier to execute.

Protective and Responsive Loss Offsets

The first type of recovery is one of the most popular. A protective and responsive loss offset contains two phases. The protective step occurs when a trader sees that a loss is possible and takes steps to prevent or mitigate it. The second is performed in response to a loss. The most prudent form is to close a position to take a small loss, avoiding a larger loss from occurring later.

Protective Offset

In the protective loss offset, a trader opens a new position to offset potential losses. A good example is a protective put. A trader owns 100 shares of stock originally purchased for $37 per share. Recently, price surged to $42, a paper profit 5 points, or $500. Now fearing the possibility of retracement, the trader sets up a protective offset by purchasing a 42 put for 3 ($300). If the underlying price declines below the strike, the put gains one point of intrinsic value for every point lost in the stock. Breakeven is at $39 per share (42–3). Because the original price paid per share was $37, this protective offset protects two points of profit above the original price paid.

Another version is the synthetic short stock trade. This combines a long put and a short call. The trader could open a synthetic short stock trade at a 42 strike for close to no cost (and perhaps even a small net credit). This protects against market risk below $42 per share, thus protecting all the paper profits gained to date.

However, because this trade involves a short call, it adds a new risk. If the price per share rises above $2 per share and the call is exercised, shares will be called away at $2 per share, no matter how high the price of the underlying moved. This is a riskless trade in two respects. First, the synthetic was opened for zero cost, so there is no options risk. Second, because the short call is covered, exercise would not create a loss, but a profit. Shares were purchased at $37 and called away at $42, a $500 profit for 100 shares.

Some may argue against the synthetic short stock, arguing that if the covered call is exercised, the potential gain on appreciated stock will be lost. However, the purpose of opening this trade was not to make more profit, but to protect the $500 paper profit already existing. The synthetic short stock trade eliminates all market risk on both sides. A decline in the underlying is offset point for point in intrinsic value of the put; a gain in the underlying allows the trader to realize the existing $500 profit. Even though the trades resolve potential losses whether the underlying rises or falls, the short call can be rolled forward to avoid or delay exercise. If it is possible to roll forward and up to a higher strike, the eventual profit is increased above $500.

Responsive Offset

The second form is responsive offset. This is a trade entered once a loss occurs and may follow a realized loss or be entered to reduce exposure in a paper loss. Unlike the protective offset in which steps are taken to anticipate and prevent a loss, the responsive offset involves acting after a loss has already occurred.

For example, early exercise of an option sets up a net loss. A responsive offset can take many forms, but its purpose is to recover the loss *without adding risk* to the position. For example, a loss on a covered call should not be offset by opening a new covered call with a strike below the basis in the underlying, in a ratio position generating more cash but adding risk or creating an uncovered straddle to get back the cash lost in the first trade.

The combined purpose of maintaining the same risk level but still recovering a loss is a preferred alternative. If this is not possible, it makes more sense to accept the loss, and move on to the next, more promising trade.

An example of a responsive offset that makes sense is replacing the loss on a covered call with an uncovered put. If a comfortable buffer zone is set up between the current price of the underlying and the strike of the put, this is a relatively safe trade. Market risk is the same as that of covered calls, but as a replacement it often accomplishes the desired goal. This assumes as well that the underlying price pattern indicates a likelihood of a price retracement, based on reversal signals and confirmation. It also is a strategy that—like most short positions—should be limited to a very short time until expiration.

Selective Rolling

Most options traders know all about rolling. When a short position has moved in the money and expiration is coming soon, the position is closed at a loss and replaced with another one expiring in the future. But is it always a wise idea, or should it be done only selectively?

Typically, the roll moves from the current expiration to the next one, and at the same strike. This sets up a net credit, which is always desirable. But another factor, often overlooked, is that this also changes the true basis in the new option.

For example, you sold a 50 call for 3 ($300) last week. It has moved in the money and now is valued at 4.25. You close this, take the $125 loss and replace it with a 50 call expiring next Friday. For this you receive a net premium of 5.50 ($550). However, the true basis in this new short call is not $550, but $425:

Net credit for new position		$550
Less: Bought to close prior position	$425	
Sold to open prior position	300	
Net loss, prior position		125
Adjusted basis, new position		$425

The prior loss is easily overlooked, but this can create a problem for the forward roll. The value at the time the position was opened was $550, but your basis in the call is $425. To set up a net credit, you must see the premium decline to below your net basis of $425.

This is possible, of course; but if it does not decline, the paper loss could grow to an even larger level. At the point of opening the new position (assuming it is at the same strike) it is already in the money, so you rely on the underlying moving low enough, so the option moves out of the money.

The point to keep in mind is that you might be better off to just take the loss and not roll forward. In the example above, your loss would be $125. Instead of rolling forward, check the premium level of next week's calls at a higher strike, one that is at or out of the money. You will receive less premium for this replacement, but it avoids exercise, whereas the forward roll cannot provide the same benefit. If a trader wants to call this a forward roll, there is no damage in doing so.

However, generally, you do not have to offset a loss at 100%, meaning getting large credit on the new position than the loss on the prior position. Accepting a small net loss in exchange for improved moneyness often is a preferable outcome.

Closing and Taking Losses

Even without a forward roll, closing an in-the-money (ITM) position and taking a loss is not a failure. In fact, it might help you avoid a larger loss. No one is going to reach 100% profitability, and the measure of success or failure should not be limited to the dollar value of all your trades, but to how well you are able to move forward after experiencing a loss.

When should you take a loss? The answer has two parts. First, always take a loss if you believe there is a possibility of the loss growing, from a small loss into a larger loss. There is no point in waiting to see when you are not certain.

Second, take a loss when it is possible to recover from the loss by opening a new position with greater potential for profits and less exposure to exercise. For example, you sold a 50 call for 1.50 a week ago. The call has moved in the money. The underlying is now at $52 per share and the call expires tomorrow. It is valued at 2.75. In this situation, with only 0.75 time value remaining, the chances for a recovery within one day are slim.

A more practical alternative is to take the loss and seek a new short call with a higher strike and higher premium. Your loss will be 1.25 (2.75–1.50). What do next week's calls and strike show? Can you find a 52.50 strike worth more than 1.25? This will be out of the money and offer more premium than your loss.

Is it realistic to expect higher premium for a one-week duration and a higher strike? Yes. For example, on Friday, August 10, 2018, Boeing (BA) closed at $343.72 per share. At that time the one-week 342.50 calls (in the money by 1.22) were at an ask price of 2.25. The two-week 345 calls were at a bid of 2.80. This means a seven-day call could be bought to close for $225, and one week later, higher strike calls could be sold to open for 2.80. This is $55 net credit, and also represents a gain of 2.5 points in the strike. In exchange, expiration takes an additional week.

In this situation, a holder of a short ITM call could avoid exercise and set up a higher strike short call expiring a week later. This is an example of good timing to take a loss and replace the short position.

You can consider this a form of rolling forward and up; of it can be viewed as closing one position and taking a loss; and replacing it with a net credit greater than the loss *and* at a higher strike. That means that if the underlying price remains in the range where it has advanced, exercise might be avoided, or if it does occur, it will save $250 of loss upon exercise.

Entering New Positions with Higher Risks

When a loss occurs, the most prudent policy is to accept the loss and enter a recovery strategy if it is possible, preferably without adding greater risks.

Some traders develop a sense of *needing* to recover a loss, even if that means increasing market risk. This is a common problem but a big mistake. This can take many forms:

1. Replacing a conservative strategy loss with a high risk and speculative position with potentially larger gains (or losses).
2. Increasing the number of options opened, especially short positions, in the belief that it is possible to offset a loss with a higher profit from more exposure.
3. Abandoning safety buffer zones and getting higher short option premium to make up for the loss.
4. Extending expiration beyond the following week to gain higher premiums, even though this means adding to exposure time.

All these practices are ill advised not only because it translates to higher risks. It also exposes you to even greater losses if the plan does not go the way you thought it would. Most important, though, is that these practices violate your risk profile and convert you from a self-defined conservative trader into a speculator.

Speculation is not for everyone, especially for conservative traders. But some come to believe that an occasional speculative trade is justified to recapture lost money on a loss. When recovery is not practical within the limits of your risk tolerance, your best alternative is to just accept the loss, learn from it and move on to the next trade.

Expanding Exposed Spread Positions

Another form of recovery is expanding exposed spread positions. For example, in the calendar spread typical of installment strategies, the loss on a short spread could be offset by opening a higher risk short spread with more contracts, extended expiration or less advantageous strike selection.

This practice, like any form of recovery based on higher risks, is not a wise move for the conservative trader. The installment strategy is a conservative approach to the hedging of market risks. However, this does not equal a guarantee of consistent profits. Because the short-term side of the trade involves short positions in either calls or puts (or both), losses will occur. A truly conservative approach to trading means being prudent about selection of strategies, strikes, expiration and proximity to resistance or support.

Being conservative also means remembering that losses do occur and being willing to accept that as part of the mix of outcomes. If you select installment positions wisely, there should be enough flexibility in the timing of LEAPS expiration, cost of the long side and selection of short contracts, so that you can survive an occasional loss without the entire strategy failing or ending up as a net loss.

Moving a reasonable spread position (or a straddle or strangle) to a higher risk position will work against the conservative ideal in the installment strategy. It could be that recovery will not always be possible. In those cases, not trying to recover (if it means greater risk) is the truly conservative method. Managing losses does not always have to mean getting back lost money; management could also mean taking no action, accepting the loss as part of the reality of options trading and moving forward to a new trade.

13

The Flexibility of Options Hedging

The options trader succeeds as a hedger upon overcoming a common perception that options represent high risk. This is not only imposed from the outside observer but may also refer to the trader's need for self-discipline.

Many self-described conservative investors may easily stray from a well-defined level of risk tolerance and take risks inappropriate based on the profile and goals of portfolio management. This problem grows from a tendency to recognize opportunities while not also recognizing the risks involved, and many traders, including professional portfolio managers, have suffered from this tendency. Successful hedging trades will remain conservative only if the trader is able to adhere to well-defined standards of which strategies to use, when to enter or exit and when to cut losses and move on to other trades.

The Hedging and Leverage Advantage

Options traders who recognize the value to options as portfolio management tools will be able to resist the "speculation temptation" and follow a carefully defined course of action.

Options provide advantages to those conservative traders desiring a hedging opportunity. Consider the risk hedge, which sets up a LEAPS put to eliminate all market risk below the selected strike. If that put is paid for with a series of short options over time, the trader does not need to be concerned with market risk under any circumstances. That alone presents a considerable benefit and addresses the most common matter of concern to anyone who buys shares of stock, the risk of a decline below basis.

The same is true for the contingent purchase, but from a different point of view. Rather than freezing risk for long stock positions, the contingent purchase allows a trader to buy stock in the future for the strike, even if the underlying price rises many points. The cost of the LEAPS call set up to provide this benefit is zero, assuming it is paid for before expiration arrives.

This leverage is a true advantage. Compared to other forms of hedging, it is much more economically advantageous. For example, the simple insurance put requires purchase of the put without offset. The true hedging is not the strike, but the strike minus the cost of the put. This is where traders face a dilemma. If they opt for a cheap put, the hedge will not last long. If they want longer term protection, the put will be expensive.

Leverage is easily calculated, and its benefits easily realized. For example, Amazon.com (AMZN) was priced at $500 per share in September 2015. Three years later, by August 2018, the price had risen to $1900, or 380% higher. Even with a 1400-point increase in value, can a trader buy a call speculatively and expect to make a profit? As of August 15, 2018, a 1900 call expiring on June 19, 2020 (674 days), was at an ask price of 345, of $34,500. Can you expect Amazon stock to grow by more than 345 points in the next 22 months? This is unknown.

However, in place of the insurance put, what happens if you enter a contingent purchase at the 1900 strike for 674 days (expirations on June 19, 2020) and plan to pay for that expensive long call with a series of short options? With the stock price at $1885 per share on August 15, you could sell a nine-day put with a strike of 1875 (10-point buffer zone) for $2745. If you repeat a transaction at the same premium value 13 times:

$$13 * 2745 = \$35,685$$

The LEAPS call would be paid for with 13 transactions at this level. It needs to occur at least once every 52 days. If you enter a trade every two weeks (14 days), and each expires worthless, the long LEAPS call with be paid for in 182 days or just over six months.

The point of this example is that as expensive as the LEAPS call is at $34,500, it would not be difficult to pay for it with a series of sold options. This leads to an evaluation of what defines any option as "expensive." Given the ease of covering the cost by selling an option every 52 days at the least, the $34,500 required for the LEAPS call is not expensive. Many lower priced options are going to be more expensive if they cannot be easily paid for over the required time.

The hedging and leverage advantages to installment strategies make the case: the "expensive" option cannot be judged by price alone, but by the level of risk. If the cost can be covered only marginally and without any problems in positions moving in the money, then an option is going to be expensive. But a higher priced option as in the preceding example is not always expensive. Given the short-term options cited and the 10-point buffer zones, chances for success are high, and given the 52-day window, if a position does move in the money, rolling forward is always a possibility. Even taking a loss is not a catastrophe, because it can be made up with the next short option position. There was plenty of time and premiums were rich enough to make this example of an installment work out with excellent levels of hedging.

Installment Variations Based on Changing Conditions

The selection of one strategy over another is not a matter of personal preference, but of conditions. For example, you might prefer uncovered puts to uncovered calls because the risk levels are vastly different.

However, if you limit your selection of a strategy, you will either miss opportunities or make trades at the worst time. For example, you open an uncovered call after the underlying price declines. You expect a retracement and to see price return to the previous range. This occurs often enough that it creates the impression of a safe trade.

What happens if price moves in the opposite direction? If the price spikes above resistance, timing is perfect for opening a short call. But if you are comfortable only with uncovered puts, the proximity of the underlying price sets up a problem. If you sell an uncovered put and price then retraces to the downside, your put will move in the money and you face a loss on the trade or exercise of the put. To avoid this risk, you may decide to wait until conditions are more favorable. Consequently, you lose half of the opportunities to trade in favorable conditions.

Variations of installment trades—especially the short-term short options—is going to be more successful if you select the strategy appropriate to price behavior. An uncovered call is higher risk than an uncovered put but risk itself is not a fixed quality to any trade. When price spikes above resistance, especially with a large price gap, chances are very high that price will retreat and fill all or part of the gap as it retreats into the previously established range.

Selection of a strategy should not be based on assumed qualities that never change. Risk is not fixed by the strategy exclusively, but on proximity and underlying price behavior as well. Does this mean an uncovered call can be lower risk than an uncovered put? Yes. In the conditions described above, with price spiking above resistance, the uncovered call makes more sense than the uncovered put. This assumes that you also find strong reversal signals and equally strong confirmation.

The idea conditions in which uncovered calls are low risk are when the spike above resistance is extreme. For example, the default of two standard deviations for the outer bands of Bollinger Bands reveals the central tendency of price. In having moved outside of two standard deviations, you know price will not remain there for long but will retreat into the band range.

Taking this a step farther, changing the two standard deviation default to three standard deviations, if price moves above the upper band or below the lower band, conditions are ideal for opening a short option—a call on the top and a put on the bottom.

Once price moves outside of three standard deviations, it is rare for price to remain there for more than one or two trading sessions. There are no 100% guarantees of how price will behave at any time, but statistically the chances for retracement are as close to complete confidence as possible. This timing removes most of the risk to the short position.

Adjusting to Sudden Price Movement

Inevitably, there comes a time in every trader's life when an underlying price moves unexpectedly. This may be a reaction to an earnings surprise, based on news or rumors, or simply a reflection of current market-wide movement. At times, an underlying price behaves in an irrational manner and cannot be explained.

Sudden price movement is always a possibility. At times, the explanation does not explain either why the extent of price movement occurred or why price did not immediately return to previous range, as usually expected. For example, Facebook (FB) dropped 46 points in a single day on July 26, 2018, as shown in Fig. 13.1.

The news about FB was negative. Earnings did not meet expectations and the company projected a slowdown in revenues for the coming year. Even so, the chart shows the classic setup for retracement: a large price gap moving opposite the trendline, a volume spike and a support level at the same approximate price as the beginning of May, two months earlier. These symp-

The Flexibility of Options Hedging   179

Fig. 13.1 Large price movement

toms anticipated a rebound in price, but one month later it had not happened.

This is a typical surprise with a very large decline in value. However, unlike what "normally" occurs—a retracement of at least some of the gap—the stock price did not react in the immediate future. What does this mean for predictability? A contrarian or swing trader would look for reversal signals and confirmation and act accordingly. Signals—and strong ones—were present at the point of the gap.

The gap itself is a strong reversal signal, and the volume spike confirms the likelihood of reversal. Earnings surprises tend to affect stock prices for a matter of days only, but not as severely as in the case of FB. A bullish engulfing signal in the first two August sessions led price to about 17 points higher; but by mid-August, most of that gain retreated to only a few points above the low price of $170 per share.

None of the expected reactions occurred. This shows that even with the best technical tools, prediction can never be trusted at 100%. Some situations do not follow the usual course, and others do but only with a significant time delay.

Reducing Risks with Long-Term Hedging

The essence of installment strategies in various forms is risk reduction. The idea is to set up future purchase or sale contractual rights while either hedging market risk on equity positions or reserving a future price per share for later purchase.

To review the two major strategies: the risk hedge is entered when the investor owns shares in the underlying, especially if those shares have appreciated in value since they were purchased. In this situation, as an investor you face a dilemma: do you sell shares to take profits now, concerned that the price may retrace and paper profits will be lost? Or do you hold on in confidence that the investment is fundamentally and technically worth keeping?

For many in this situation, buying an insurance put is one solution that mitigates potential loss. The put eliminates market risk below the net basis (price paid for 100 shares minus premium paid for the put). This protection remains in effect until the put expires.

The insurance put is unsatisfactory because its life will be limited, and the longer the life the higher the cost, therefore the lower the net level of insurance.

The second installment strategy is the contingent purchase. In this case, if you do not own shares but would like to purchase them at the current price, buying a LEAPS call freezes the price of 100 shares. You can exercise this call before expiration and buy shares, or if the price rises, you can sell the call and take a profit. If the underlying price declines, your loss will be limited to the price paid for the long call.

Both strategies have merit but are limited. Therefore, both situations have the second component, the repetitive sale of extremely short-term short calls or puts. This should occur over a one-week to two-week period when time decay will be accelerated. It is also desirable to create a buffer zone between current price and the higher call strike or lower put strike. This enables you to buy to close the position before it moves in the money. Finally, the selection of a short call or put depends on recent price patterns. If the price of the underlying has approached or moved through resistance, selling a call is well timed. If the underlying has declined to or moved below support, selling a put makes sense.

These timing suggestions assume that the price will remain reliably within the established trading range. This will mean that the combination of time decay and reliance on resistance and support add considerable safety to the strategy.

Even so, every trader will experience losses. With short options, movement in the money is treated as a candidate for rolling forward or can be closed to cut losses or to take small profits. But losses are inevitable, which emphasizes the need to enter installment positions with a comfortable margin of both time and cost. If the breakeven requires week-to-week profits with no room for delay, it might not be possible to end up with a net profit. The less often you need to execute the short trade, the greater the chance of success. Market momentum shifts constantly, so the more flexibility you create, the more desirable it will be. This also makes it easier to time entry and exit on the short side of the transaction.

Installment hedging is not often discussed in the world of options. It requires monitoring and the ability to make decisions quickly, and patient consistency to gradually use short profits to pay the long premium. Done correctly, the installment creates a desirable condition: a long call or put with a net zero basis (created through the periodic sale of short options). This translates to great flexibility to exercise or sell the long option or, when the underlying price does not create in-the-money results, to allow the long option to expire. Because the basis will be paid down to a net zero, worthless expiration is not as severe a result as it is not a single long option without the short offsets.

The purpose of the installment strategy should be kept in mind when deciding which short positions to open. In a recovery strategy after a loss, it is equally important to avoid replacement of a loss with as higher profit and more risk. There are times when losses must be accepted so you can move forward to the next trade and not need to look back.

Many recovery strategies enable you to offset losses, but if risks are kept at a conservative level, the problems of converting small losses into larger ones can be avoided. The successful installment strategy will be based on observing these rules: time the trades based on recent price movement and identification of reversal signals. Do not increase risk exposure to offset losses. And create installments to eliminate market risk and grant yourself maximum flexibility to create future profits.

Bibliography

Alexander, C. (2008). *Market risk analysis, pricing, hedging and trading financial instruments*. Hoboken: Wiley.
An, Y., & Suo, W. (2009, Winter). An empirical comparison of option-pricing models in hedging exotic options. *Financial Management, 38*(4), 889–914.
Augen, J. (2009). *Trading options at expiration*. Upper Saddle River: Pearson Education.
Bagehot, W. (1971, March–April). The only game in town. *Financial Analysts Journal, 27*, 12–22.
Bernstein, L., & Siegel, J. (1979). The concept of earnings quality. *Financial Analysts Journal, 35*(4), 72–75.
Black, F. (1980). The magic in earnings: Economic earnings versus accounting earnings. *Financial Analysts Journal, 36*(4), 19–24.
Blume, L., Easley, D., & O'Hara, M. (1994). Market statistics and technical analysis: The role of volume. *The Journal of Finance, 49*(1), 153–181.
Bollinger, J. (1992, January). Using Bollinger Bands. *Stocks & Commodities, 10*(2), 47–51.
Bulkowski, T. (2008). *Encyclopedia of candlestick charts*. Hoboken: Wiley.
Caginalp, G., & Laurent, H. (1998, February). The predictive power of price patterns. *Applied Mathematical Finance, 5*, 3–4.
Chen, N., Grundy, B., & Stambaugh, R. (1990, January). Changing risk, changing risk premiums, and dividend yield effects. *The Journal of Business, 63*(1), 51–70.
Chung, K., Seongkyu, G., & Doojin, R. (2016, July). Trade duration, informed trading, and option moneyness. *International Review of Economics & Finance, 44*, 395–411.
Cohen, G. (2005). *The bible of options strategies: The definitive guide for practical trading strategies*. Upper Saddle River: FT Press.

© The Author(s) 2018
M. C. Thomsett, *Options Installment Strategies*,
https://doi.org/10.1007/978-3-319-99864-0

Bibliography

Coval, J., & Shumway, T. (2001, June). Expected option returns. *The Journal of Finance, 56*(3), 983–1009.

Dechow, P., Hutton, A., Meulbroek, L., & Sloan, R. (2001, July). Short-sellers, fundamental analysis, and stock returns. *Journal of Financial Economics, 61*(1), 77–106.

Dutt, T., & Humphery-Jenner, M. (2013, March). Stock return volatility, operating performance and stock returns: International evidence on drivers of the 'low volatility' anomaly. *Journal of Banking & Finance, 37*(3), 999–1017.

Emir, S., Dinçer, H., & Timor, M. (2012, August). A stock selection model based on fundamental and technical analysis variables by using artificial neural networks and support vector machines. *Review of Economics & Finance, 2*, 106–122.

Fielitz, B. (1971). On the random walk hypothesis. *The American Economist, 15*(1), 105–107.

Garg, B. (2014, October). Technical analysis indicators: Pathway towards rewarding journey. *International Journal of Management and Social Sciences Research, 3*(10), 87–93.

Gilster, J. (1997). Option pricing theory: Is 'Risk-Free' hedging feasible? *Financial Management, 26*(1), 91–105.

Green, T., & Figlewski, S. (1999). Market risk and model risk for a financial institution writing options. *The Journal of Finance, 54*(4), 1465–1500.

Greenleaf, R. (1989). Synthetic instruments. *Financial Analysts Journal, 45*(2), 71–73.

Guiso, L., Sapienza, P., & Zingales, L. (2008). Trusting the stock market. *The Journal of Finance, 63*(6), 2557–2600.

Hagin, R. (2003). *Investment management*. Hoboken: Wiley.

Hao, J., Kalay, A., & Mayhew, S. (2010). Ex-dividend arbitrage in option markets. *The Review of Financial Studies, 23*(1), 271–303.

Hentschel, L., & Kothari, S. (2001). Are corporations reducing or taking risks with derivatives? *The Journal of Financial and Quantitative Analysis, 36*(1), 93–118.

Hobbs, R. (2017). *Create to learn: Introduction to digital literacy*. Hoboken: Wiley-Blackwell.

Hoffland, D. (1967, May–June). The Folklore of Wall Street. *Financial Analysts Journal, 23*(3), 85–88.

Hoffmann, A., & Shefrin, H. (2014). Technical analysis and individual investors. *Journal of Economic Behavior & Organization, 107*, 487–511.

Hwang, S., & Satchell, S. (2000, May). Market risk and the concept of fundamental volatility: Measuring volatility across asset and derivative markets and testing for the impact of derivatives markets on financial markets. *Journal of Banking & Finance, 24*(5), 759–785.

Jong, C., Koedijk, K., & Schnitzlein, C. (2006, July). Stock market quality in the presence of a traded option. *The Journal of Business, 79*(4), 2243–2274.

Kuprianov, A. (1995, Fall). Derivatives debacle. *Economic Quarterly, 81*(4), 1–39.

Lee, C., & Swaminathan, B. (2000, October). Price momentum and trading volume. *The Journal of Finance, LV*(5), 2017–2069.

Levy, R. (1966). Conceptual foundations of technical analysis. *Financial Analysts Journal, 22*(4), 83–89.

Levy, R. A. (1971). The predictive significance of five-point chart patterns. *The Journal of Business, 44*(3), 316–323.

Loh, R., & Warachka, M. (2012). Streaks in earnings surprises and the cross-section of stock returns. *Management Science, 58*(7), 1305–1321.

Manley, R., & Mueller-Glissmann, C. (2008). The market for dividends and related investment strategies. *Financial Analysts Journal, 64*(3), 17–29.

McMillan, L. (2002). *Options as a strategic investment* (4th ed.). New York: New York Institute of Finance.

Merton, R., Scholes, M., & Gladstein, M. (1978). The returns and risk of alternative call option portfolio investment strategies. *The Journal of Business, 51*(2), 183–242.

Mueller, P. (1981). Covered options: An alternative investment strategy. *Financial Management, 10*(4), 64–71.

Natenberg, S. (1994). *Option volatility & pricing*. New York: McGraw-Hill.

Nison, S. (2001). *Japanese candlestick charting techniques* (2nd ed.). New York: New York Institute of Finance.

Northcott, A. (2009). *The complete guide to using candlestick charting*. Ocala: Atlantic Publishing Group.

Passarelli, D. (2011). *The Market Taker's Edge: Insider Strategies from the Options Trading Floor*. New York: McGraw-Hill Education.

Pozen, R. (1978). The purchase of protective puts by financial institutions. *Financial Analysts Journal, 34*(4), 47–60.

Rhoads, R. (2011). *Option spread trading: A comprehensive guide to strategies and tactics*. Hoboken: Wiley.

Roll, R., Schwartz, E., & Avanidhar, S. (2010, April). O/S: The relative trading activity in options and stock. *Journal of Financial Economics, 96*(1), 1–17.

Snyder, G. (1967, January–February). A look at options. *Financial Analysts Journal, 23*(1), 100–103.

Tabell, E., & Tabell, A. (1964, March–April). The case for technical analysis. *Financial Analysts Journal, 20*(2), 67–76.

Index[1]

A
Accounting rules, 43–45
Accumulation/distribution (A/D), 61
Advantageous price levels, 4–6
Amazon.com, 84, 176
Annual trends, 33
AT&T, 84
At the money (ATM), 17, 18, 84, 115, 117, 118, 125, 150–152, 154

B
Black candle, 25, 61
Black-Scholes pricing model, 3
Blue-chip stocks, 42, 53
Boeing (BA), 171
Bollinger Bands, 5, 6, 13, 21, 22, 49, 53–56, 97, 99–101, 128, 129, 132, 135, 157, 158, 178
Box synthetic, 110
Breakaway gap, 56, 57
Breakout, 4, 10, 11, 19, 20, 24–26, 52, 53, 56, 61, 130

Buffer zone, 72, 76, 77, 102–105, 117, 136, 147, 152–154, 157, 165, 169, 172, 176, 177
Butterfly, 118–120, 137

C
Calendar spread, 27, 35, 153, 172
Candlestick continuation, 60–61
Candlestick reversal, 8, 24, 56, 59–60
Candlesticks (Eastern), 8–10
Chevron (CVX), 84, 150
Chicago Board Options Exchange (CBOE), 28
Chipotle (CMG), 102–104, 112, 113
Citigroup (C), 46
Coca-Cola (KO), 40
Collateral requirements, 27–28
Common gap, 51, 56
Condor, 118, 137
Confirmation, vii, 5, 6, 10–12, 19, 20, 23, 24, 50, 51, 56, 59, 60, 62, 64, 97, 101, 102, 123, 126, 130, 169, 178, 179

---

[1]Note: Page numbers followed by 'n' refer to notes.

© The Author(s) 2018
M. C. Thomsett, *Options Installment Strategies*,
https://doi.org/10.1007/978-3-319-99864-0

187

Confirmation bias, 51, 69–70
Conservative investors, v, 175
Consolidation trends, 24–26, 53, 57, 76, 115, 125
Contingent purchase, vii, 28, 35–37, 81–91, 95–98, 100, 101, 107, 120, 121, 124, 133, 139, 144, 145, 147, 152, 157, 176, 180
Contingent sales, 37–39
Continuation, vii, 5, 8–11, 20, 23, 24, 49–51, 56, 57, 59–61, 64
Contrarian, 70, 164, 179
Covered call, vi, 28, 34, 76, 77, 94–96, 98–101, 110, 115, 131, 133, 141, 143, 148, 156–158, 163, 168, 169
Covered straddle, 115–117, 148–150
Covered strangle, 76, 77, 117
Credit spread, 111–114
Cum-dividend, 160, 161
Current price proximity, 123–127

D

Debit spread, 111
Debt capitalization, 3, 71
Debt to total capitalization ratio, 33, 40–43, 71
Delta, 17
Diagonal spread, 27, 95, 111–115
Dividend capture, 160, 161
Dividend per share, 33, 39–41, 43, 45, 71, 121
Dividend yield, 33, 39–40, 43, 71, 121
Doji star, 127
Double hedge, 95, 96
Double top and bottom, 11, 23, 57
Dow Theory, 11, 22

E

Early exercise, 27, 143, 161, 169
Earnings surprise, 12, 34, 70, 76, 161–164, 178, 179
Earnings week, 161–164

Eastman Kodak, 42
eBay, 102, 104
Effects of fundamental trends, 33–35
Eight new price lines signal, 25
Engulfing, 6, 60, 127, 179
Entering new positions, 172
Entry and exit timing, 3, 6, 13, 14, 26, 32, 50–51, 61, 63, 64, 68, 102, 104, 105, 108, 123, 124, 127, 130, 132, 181
Ex-dividend, 27, 160–161
Exercise, 20, 27–29, 34, 38, 39, 73, 76–78, 81, 85, 86, 88–89, 91, 93–98, 100, 101, 105, 114, 117, 125, 126, 128, 132, 133, 136, 137, 140–143, 147, 149, 152–154, 157, 159–162, 168–171, 177, 180, 181
Exhaustion gap, 56, 57
Exposed spread positions, 172–173
Extrinsic value, 77

F

Facebook (FB), 144–146, 148, 178, 179
Federal Trade Commission (FTC), 70
Fedex (FDX), 102, 115–118
Flexibility, vii, 88, 120, 148, 149, 154, 157, 159, 173, 175–181
Forward roll, 73, 105, 140, 170, 171
Fundamental risk, 32–33
Fundamental volatility, 3, 4, 32–35, 37, 44, 82

G

GAAP system, 45
Gambler's fallacy, 162
Gamma, 17
Gap filled, 60
Gaps, 2, 4, 10, 11, 19, 23, 24, 34, 49, 56–58, 60, 61, 96–98, 101, 112, 129, 130, 142, 145, 157, 158, 162, 177–179

Generally Accepted Accounting Principles (GAAP), 45
General Mills, 86
General Motors (GM), 37, 42

H

Harami, 5, 51, 60, 127
Head and shoulders, 11, 23
Hedging, vi–viii, 1, 2, 15–17, 28, 31, 37, 65, 67, 69, 84, 107, 139, 140, 154, 155, 173, 175–181
Helmerich & Payne (HP), 131
Historical volatility (HV), 1, 3, 4, 13, 22, 34, 35, 37, 52, 53, 128–130
Horizontal spread, 35, 95

I

IBM, 98–100, 142, 143
Implied volatility (IV), 1–3, 12–14, 18, 33, 35, 77, 128
Informed investor, 16, 96
Installment strategy, vii, 6, 10, 13, 15, 19, 27–29, 31, 32, 37, 42, 43, 46, 49, 50, 61, 65, 87, 93, 94, 96, 101, 102, 105, 107, 111, 120, 121, 128, 136, 137, 139, 140, 150, 151, 153–155, 159, 161, 163, 165, 172, 173, 177, 180, 181
Installment variations, 177–178
Insurance put, vii, 71, 78, 79, 176, 180
Internet, 9, 20, 67
In the money (ITM), 17, 18, 27, 28, 34, 38, 72, 73, 76, 88, 93, 98–100, 105, 114, 117, 125, 126, 128, 140, 141, 143, 147, 149, 150, 152–154, 156, 159–162, 169–171, 177, 180, 181
Intrinsic value, 18, 38, 71, 77–79, 81, 85, 86, 91, 95, 98, 100, 117, 132, 139, 142, 147, 150, 152, 153, 159, 164, 168, 169

Iron butterfly, 118–120
Island cluster, 23, 58, 130

J

Japanese candlestick, 8, 9, 59
Johnson & Johnson, 82, 83

K

Key to profitable trades, 2–4
Kodak, 37
Kohl's, 86
Kraft Heinz, 82, 83

L

LEAPS option, vii, 19, 26, 67, 89, 118, 132, 141, 146
Levels of risk, 93–105, 107
Leverage, 107, 109, 132, 175–177
Lockheed Martin (LMT), 44, 45, 89, 90
Locking in the future price, 81–84
Long puts, 4, 7, 19, 22, 37, 71–79, 89, 141–144, 168
Long-term contingent purchase, 81–91, 145
Long-term hedging, 180–181
Long-term long put, 72–74

M

Margin calculator, 28
Margin requirement, 28, 153
Market momentum, 181
Market risk, v–viii, 1, 2, 4, 7, 13, 15–17, 28–29, 31, 32, 36–39, 65, 67–79, 93, 94, 100, 110, 115, 117, 120, 121, 125, 128, 133, 134, 139, 142, 148, 149, 157, 164, 165, 168, 169, 172, 173, 175, 180, 181
McDonalds (MCD), 42, 43

Meeting lines, 127
Microsoft (MSFT), 44, 45, 148, 149
MMM, 133, 135
Momentum, viii, 2, 4–6, 10, 12, 13, 22, 23, 50, 56, 57, 59, 62–63, 97, 126, 130
Money flow index (MFI), 61
Moneyness, 16–18, 22, 23, 96, 102, 125, 159–160, 170
Moving average convergence/divergence (MACD), 62
Moving average (MA), 5, 6, 10, 12, 13, 23, 50, 53, 54, 56, 59, 62, 64–65, 126, 158
Multiple increments, 136–137

N
Naked option, 99
Nature of underlying risk, 68–71
Netflix (NFLX), 91
Nison, Steve, 20
Non-price signals, 11–12

O
OHLC chart, 9, 10
On balance volume (OBV), 61
Options and market risk, 28–29
Options Clearing Corporation (OCC), 160
Out of the money (OTM), 17, 18, 76, 95, 96, 98–100, 102–104, 113–115, 117, 118, 126, 142, 146–149, 159, 163, 170, 171

P
Pacific Gas & Electric, 40
Perfect hedge, 67, 75
Positions with higher risks, 172
Price/earnings (P/E) ratio, 3, 33, 44–46, 71

Price patterns, 2, 6–8, 23, 24, 55, 56, 118, 169, 180
Price proximity, 102–104, 123–127
Protective offset, 168–169
Protective put, 71, 72, 168
Proximity, vi–viii, 4, 8, 11, 14–29, 34, 51, 59, 76, 99–105, 110, 111, 123–127, 157–160, 164, 165, 173, 177, 178
Proximity in consolidation trends, 24–26
Proximity of price to resistance or support, 19–22, 159
Proximity to expiration, 18–19

R
Random walk hypothesis (RWH), 20, 55, 68
Ratio write, 76, 98–100, 136, 163
Recovery strategy, viii, 155, 167–173, 181
Reducing risk exposure, 159–160
Relative strength index (RSI), 5, 12, 62, 63, 129, 130, 145
Resistance, 4, 6, 10, 11, 19–26, 49, 51–57, 59, 76, 99, 102, 111, 118, 123–128, 130, 132, 135, 142, 143, 157–159, 165, 173, 177, 178, 180
Responsive offset, 169
Retracement, 10, 26, 50, 51, 55, 82, 132, 135, 143, 145, 157, 158, 162–165, 168, 169, 177–179
Revenue and earnings trends, 33, 35, 45–46
Reversal, vii, 5, 6, 8–13, 19, 20, 22–27, 34, 35, 49–52, 54–64, 68, 69, 97, 100–102, 105, 123, 126–127, 129, 130, 132, 135, 145, 158, 169, 178, 179, 181

Index

Risk elimination, 67–79, 86–88
Risk hedge, v–vii, 15–17, 28, 32, 37–39, 65, 67–79, 84–86, 89, 94–96, 98–101, 105, 107, 120, 121, 124–126, 132, 133, 137, 139, 141–144, 147, 148, 152, 175, 180
Risk in every strategy, 26–27
Risk profile, v, vii, 99, 100, 155, 172
Risk transfer, 1
Rolling forward, 34, 73, 75, 93, 105, 141, 170, 171, 177, 181
Rounded top and bottom, 11, 23, 57–59
Runaway gap, 56, 57

S

Sears Holding (SHLD), 41, 42
Selective rolling, 169–170
Short options, vii, 4, 7, 10, 13, 19, 26, 27, 31, 36, 39, 50, 65, 72–74, 76, 78, 79, 84, 86–89, 91, 93–105, 111, 112, 117, 118, 120, 121, 123, 126, 130, 131, 133, 135–137, 139–141, 145, 150, 152–154, 156, 157, 159, 161–163, 172, 175–178, 181
Short positions at risk, 156–158
Short-term expiration advantages, 165
Short-term short positions, 19, 26, 27, 72–74, 114, 128, 136
Speculation, 1, 155, 156, 172, 175
Standard deviation, 13, 53, 97–99, 101, 128, 129, 132, 178
Stock selection, vii, 14n5, 32, 35–39, 70, 86, 94
Straddles, 76, 89, 95, 105, 107, 115–118, 120, 130, 131, 137, 144–150, 169, 173
Strangles, 76, 77, 115–118, 130, 137, 144–150, 173
Strap and strip, 150–152

Strongest reversal proximity, 22–24
Strong fundamental trends, 12–14, 35
Sudden price movement, 178–179
Support, 4, 6, 10, 11, 14n5, 19–24, 26, 37, 49, 51–56, 59, 76, 102, 118, 123–128, 132, 143, 145, 158, 159, 165, 173, 178, 180
Swing trades, viii, 8, 54, 59, 120, 135, 165
Synthetic stock, 107–111, 132, 134, 135

T

Taking losses, 171
Target (TGT), 108, 109
Technical indicators, 1–3, 37
Technical risk, 32
Tesla (TSLA), 118, 119, 163, 164
Three black crows, 6, 60
Three white soldiers, 127
Thrusting lines, 60
Time decay, 18, 19, 72, 74, 76, 81, 87, 96, 98, 104–105, 114, 115, 117, 118, 120, 126, 133, 136, 137, 139, 144, 147–150, 153, 158–159, 163–165, 180
Time spread, 35–38
Time value, 19, 36, 78, 81, 89, 91, 100, 101, 104, 115, 142, 143, 157, 158, 161, 165, 171
T-line, 49, 54–56, 128, 158
Triangles, 11, 51, 60

U

Unavoidable risks, 93–94
Uncovered calls, v, 34, 95–98, 101, 111, 157, 158, 177, 178
Uncovered puts, 76, 77, 95–97, 100, 101, 111, 115, 131, 148, 157–158, 169, 177, 178

Index

Underlying risk, 68–71
Unexpected events, 70
Uninformed investor, 16

V

Value investment, 31, 46
Variable ratio write, 76, 99, 163
Verizon (VZ), 73, 74
Vertical spread, 111
Volume, 5, 6, 10–13, 16, 23, 49, 50, 56, 59, 61–62, 97, 101, 126, 129, 130, 145, 178, 179
Volume spike, 5, 6, 12, 23, 61, 62, 97, 101, 129, 130, 145, 178, 179

W

Walmart (WMT), 43
Wedges, 11, 51, 60
Wells Fargo (WFC), 46
Western price indicators, 10–11
White candle, 25
Wing spreads, 118